No More
Letter of the Week

Pat Lusche

Published by: Crystal Springs Books
A division of Staff Development for Educators
10 Sharon Road, PO Box 500
Peterborough, NH 03458
1-800-321-0401
www.crystalsprings.com
www.sde.com

© 2003 Pat Lusche
Published 2003
Printed in the United States of America

08   07   06   3   4   5

ISBN-13: 978-1-884548-49-9
ISBN-10: 1-884548-49-0

Library of Congress Cataloging-in-Publication Data

Lusche, Pat.
  No more letter of the week : a framework for integrating reading
strategies and cueing systems with letter-sound instruction / by Pat
Lusche.
    p. cm
  ISBN 1-884548-49-0
  1. Reading (Kindergarten)—Handbooks, manuals, etc. 2.
Reading—Phonetic method—Handbooks, manuals, etc. I. Title.
  LB1181.25.L87 2003
  372.41-dc21

2003000830

Editor: Meredith A. Reed O'Donnell
Art Director, Designer, and Production Coordinator: Soosen Dunholter
Publishing Projects Coordinator: Deborah Fredericks
Illustrator: Phyllis Pittet

Dedication

his book is dedicated to Linda Swain, a friend and colleague who implemented this framework, continually urged me to write this guidebook, and paved the way to publication.

Contents

Preface

As kindergarten teachers we face a unique and important challenge: We are the gentle beginning of public education; we are the "first impression" for eager and not-so-eager parents. It is critical that each child experiences success at this early stage in her/his educational career and that the parents of our students feel welcome as partners in this learning adventure. Ours is a huge responsibility. And with professional and academic expectations continuously on the rise for teachers and students across the nation, the challenge, for half-day kindergarten sessions in particular, is how to accomplish more each year within the same limited amount of time. My response to this challenge, at least for my classroom literacy program, is this book.

No More Letter of the Week provides an efficient framework for introducing letter-sounds while concurrently promoting reading and writing. I have made a strong effort to safeguard developmentally appropriate practices, while also making changes that reflect good research. Section 1 of this guidebook explains the rationale for and breaks down the implementation of this framework. Section 2 takes a closer look at other literacy components in the kindergarten classroom.

Students at this age are a magic mix of giggles, questions, innocence, hugs, and excitement. Literacy and our little ones—a great place to invest our energies!

About the Author

Pat Lusche has spent the majority of her 20 years in education as a kindergarten classroom teacher. She teaches in Colorado at Cimarron Elementary School for the Cherry Creek School District. Currently, she is a reading specialist who runs a reading lab for at-risk readers in first and second grades.

Pat is the first recipient of Staff Development for Educator's I Teach K Award (2000), honoring her for exemplary teaching practices. She is also the author of the emergent reader *The Inside Story* (Dominie Press, 1996). As a member of a Public Education and Business Coalition (PEBC) scholar's group, Pat and fellow group members published "Teacher-Researchers Study the Process of Synthesizing in Six Primary Classrooms," an article that appeared in the December 1996 edition of *Language Arts*. The research conducted by the scholar's group led to speaking engagements at the Colorado Council of International Reading Association (CCIRA) and National Council of Teachers of English (NCTE) conferences. In 1992 the Kellogg Foundation awarded Pat and a colleague a grant to implement a forty-student multiage classroom in an effort to improve reading scores. Pat has served her district by helping to plan literacy conferences, teaching staff development classes, and conducting classroom teaching labs.

Pat is a wife and proud mother of two incredible sons. When time permits, she and her husband can be found at the family cabin in the Rockies, dreaming of having grandchildren.

Acknowledgments

I am forever grateful to national literacy expert Marie Clay for providing educators with such in-depth research and useful information to help us better understand emergent literacy.

I cannot thank Mary Berrington enough for her academic rigor and insightful training. She has been such a strong and treasured leader in the Cherry Creek School District.

Thanks to my many students, who continually lead the way by forcing me to direct and refine my instruction. *They* are the best teachers!

I am blessed with a principal, Jim McDermott, who supports my efforts, allowing me to job-share and adjust my hours to accommodate my writing.

I work with a talented team of kindergarten teachers, GiGi Boryla, Cyndy Harding-McBee, and Sandy Holtegel. Thanks to them for implementing the framework and supplying me with valuable input and constant support and encouragement.

I thank Steph Harvey, who through the Public Education and Business Coalition formed a scholars group of teachers from different school districts in Colorado. This powerful contingent led me through the experiences of research and publication and shared its strength, something from which I continually draw.

Thank-you to Laura Benson, the most literary person I know, who has generously shared wisdom, inspiration, and a poetic love of words.

Thanks to Frank Lloyd Kramer for his generous gift of time. He managed to rework the Sound Card rhymes while simultaneously publishing his latest book, *From the Theater of My Mind* (Castle Publishing, 2002).

And finally, a big thanks to my dear husband, Jim, who contributed his enthusiasm, adjusted his social life, and brought me warm cookies when I needed them most.

Introduction

*P*aint pigs pink. Prepare potato pancakes. Pitch pine cones. Put poems in your pocket, and meet me outside for a party in the park to celebrate Pp Week . . . . Perfect! After 26 well-planned weeks honoring each of our 26 glorious letters, most of my students knew their letters and sounds. (I'm sure the nine students who *already* knew all their letters and sounds had a good time, too.) And planning, no problem: Pull a *Pp* ditto sheet; plan a step-by-step pumpkin art project; and take time for a little free-play.

As a veteran kindergarten teacher, I am amazed at the limited amount of information I used to share with my kindergartners about the actual reading process. Fortunately, with time, experience, and the research-based guidance of gifted educators such as Cambourne, Holdaway, and Graves—just to name a few—my literacy instruction began to take a different form.

Realizing that a fascination with rich literature across many genres would capture and entice these promising readers, I made literature an integral part of class. I started using big books to model letters, sounds, concepts about print, and reading strategies; journal writing and publishing became learning adventures as students eagerly worked to produce their own published books to share with friends and family; publishers began providing an exciting assortment of books suitable for emergent readers. The children were energized, engaged, and taking a more active role in their learning, and I was being lulled into a state of satisfaction and comfort, until . . . .

Reading Recovery®: Avalanche of New Information

Assimilating new information from my Reading Recovery® training made me question my entire literacy curriculum, in particular how I introduced letters and sounds to my kindergartners. For years I had been emphasizing and isolating letters and sounds while ignoring or postponing important reading strategies and cueing systems implicit to my students' engagement in the magical process of reading. The students simply weren't receiving enough supported practice. To use a basketball analogy (as a six-foot-tall mother of two boys is inclined to do), it was as if I, as the coach, had taught the team to shoot the ball through the hoop, but had neglected to inform them about positions, dribbling, passing, game plays, and rules. My "team" of students possessed a very important isolated skill, but they couldn't "play" the game.

Marie Clay's research, writings, and Reading Recovery® program supply invaluable information and strategies for supporting emergent readers and writers, and her work continually serves as a filter through which I closely examine how I approach literacy instruction.

Persistent Questions

"Smooth seas do not make skillful sailors," goes an African proverb, so although I felt my classroom literacy program was better informed and more engaging than ever, additional training nonetheless continued to make me rethink what I was teaching and how I was teaching it. Following are four questions that disrupted the "peaceful waters" of my literacy instruction, ultimately leading to the creation of my letter-sound framework and *No More Letter of the Week*.

I. Is it an efficient use of classroom time to introduce letters and sounds in isolation?

Children (*and* adults, for that matter) will learn something much faster if they have an immediate use for that knowledge. It is important for students to excerpt letters, sounds, or words from a text, examine them, and return them to the context of the original text from which they were taken. Young pianists don't sit and memorize notes; they start by learning to play simple songs in conjunction with learning individual notes. Sixteen-year-olds don't practice isolated driving skills; they drive around the block with supervision until they gradually refine their driving skills. Learning to speak French while living in France will be more effective than learning French in a classroom setting. The immediate application of knowledge promotes retention of that knowledge.

Reading Recovery® founder Marie Clay (1991) describes four sets of behaviors students must exhibit in order to gain control over printed language. These behaviors are governed by serial order and include the following:

- Visual attention to print. The reader needs to decide what s/he will attend to and in what order (looking at the letters, or letter clusters, words, sentences, etc.).

- Directional behavior. Readers must make automatic the process of following text left to right, top to bottom, and doing a return sweep at the end of a line.

- Talking like a book. Book language sounds different than spoken language. Children, through experience, learn language patterns—the order of words—that are familiar to books (e.g., ". . . *said the frog.*").

- Hearing sounds in sequences of language. When blending sounds across unknown words, they must retain the serial order of those sounds (e.g., *a . . . b . . . ou . . . t* spells *about,* not *touab*).

Clay explains, "for success in reading[,] all these behaviors must become part of an action system which allows for smooth sequential decision-making as the young reader moves through the messages of continuous text. To begin reading instruction by teaching letters in isolation is to eliminate the role of serial order altogether and dodge the crucial problem."

The "crucial problem" to which Clay refers is not identifying letters but "extracting information from embedded letters while reading for meaning," the real learning goal.

Students should integrate cueing systems and strategies (see Appendix A, page 84) from the beginning. Provide "lively examples of the skill in action" (Holdaway 1979)—an important tenet to appropriate developmental learning—to ensure a smoother, faster transition to independent reading.

Letter-sound introduction should be more closely linked to the entire reading process.

2. What about the students who already know their letters and sounds? What are they learning while I'm doing "whole-class" letter-sound introduction?

Squirming Justin, who can read at a first-grade level, makes it difficult for me to continue with whole-class letter-sound introduction. I look into his eyes and feel his desire for academic stimulation, too.

Educators such as Clay (1991) discuss the importance of being on the "cutting" edge of each child's learning, teaching efficiently what it is individual students need to know next. It is counterproductive, for some students, to be participating in whole-class instruction that offers only previously mastered information. Jan Richardson (2000) addressed this issue by speaking about the importance of the "window you teach through." You must open your window wide enough to meet the needs of all your learners. When letters and sounds are introduced, there has to be something in it for everyone, reader and nonreader.

Former Russian psychologist and philosopher Lev Vygotsky developed the zone of proximal development (ZPD). Dixon-Krauss (1996) shares the following about Vygotsky and his definition of the ZPD:

> Vygotsky believed that good instruction is aimed at the learner's zone of proximal development. He describes the zone of proximal development as encompassing the gap between the child's level of *actual development*, determined by independent problem solving, and her level of *potential development*, determined by problem solving supported by an adult or through collaboration with more capable peers (Vygotsky 1978, 1986).

In simple terms, the ZPD is the gap between what a student already knows and what s/he can do with help. The most efficient teaching occurs in a child's zone of proximal development. And the most successful program is one that allows "children to enter at different levels" (Clay 1991).

Guided reading and guided writing offer individualization that meets students at their level. Like guided reading and guided writing, letter-sound introduction should also attend to all ability levels.

3. Are my students spending enough time practicing guided and independent reading? It seems I am spending too much time modeling and talking. There should be a better balance among modeled reading, shared reading, guided reading, and independent reading.

The bell rings, and we're off. A mother needs a mini-conference before she departs; the story took a little longer than expected; the intercom announces the forgotten assembly; and before you know it the day is over. There is never enough time! Often in this rush, the activities that get shortened or cancelled are those that are most important—such as the time children explore literacy. I need a systematic way of protecting the time students practice what I model.

Writes Richard Allington, "Engagement in reading has been found to be the most powerful instructional activity for fostering reading growth" (2001). He suggests that 90 minutes per day should be spent reading in the elementary grades—students "actually reading"—not teachers providing reading instruction, not activities to promote reading, but ACTUAL READING. Although many kindergarten programs are only half-day, and although students at this age are just learning to read, the importance of them *actually reading* should not be diminished.

Marie Clay writes about curriculum components that will open doors to literacy and components that will close doors. She tells us that the quickest way to close the door to literacy is by preventing students from "conduct[ing] the or-chestra—not being allowed to put it all together for himself or herself " (1998).

4. With ever-escalating district and state expectations, how can I increase the reading levels of my students by the end of the year and still respect and protect their need for developmentally appropriate practices?

This was the final question that led me to develop the framework for introducing letters and sounds to kindergartners presented in this book. I had to find a way to incorporate everything I know about the way children learn with *every* portion of my students' day. Letter-sound introduction had to change! And, I am happy to report, it did!

Informed Changes for Letters-Sounds Introduction

The Goal: Develop a framework for introducing letters and sounds that reflects current research about emergent literacy and more closely aligns with other literacy components in a balanced-literacy program.

Letter-sound instruction should:

- be orchestrated with the reading process, rather than be a prerequisite to the reading process

- incorporate developmentally appropriate practices and safeguard the "fun" inherently associated with kindergarten

- take into consideration the learning needs of all students, from the student who knows only one letter to the student who is already reading

- blend with other cueing systems and reading strategies to promote students' understanding of the relationship among letters, sounds, words, sentences, and the reading process

- systematically provide sufficient modeling, scaffolding, and independent practice

- include assessment

As a lab teacher and presenter I have shared this framework with many educators, and I am pleased to report its success. Please keep in mind, however, that this book is not intended to be a complete reading program; it is simply a framework for introducing letters and sounds that will serve as a resource to support independent, happy readers. It is also important that I complete an organized recording of my thoughts. As one of my observant kindergartners recently told me (as I was frantically looking for yet another misplaced item), "Mrs. Lusche, I think you're losin' your remembrin'."

Letter-Sounds

Using a series of Sound Cards, you will be introducing 35 sounds:

- Two sounds for each vowel (except for *y*)

- Twenty-one consonant sounds (note that some consonants take on other sounds—e.g., *c* can make the /k/ sound or the /s/ sound)

- Four digraphs (*th, sh, ch, wh*)

A formal introduction to written language should be kept simple and accessible to the young learner. For the majority of kindergartners, limiting mastery of two sounds per vowel is sufficient. The more complex facets of our language (other phonemes, *y* acting as a vowel in the middle and end of words, *r* controlled vowels, etc.) can be shared as needed in guided reading.

Timeframe and Letter-Sound Order

Although your timeframe can be flexible, I suggest you introduce all Sound Cards within the first four to eight weeks of school. Start with "high-utility" letters—letters students are apt to encounter more often in their reading and writing, such as *r* and *s* (versus *x* and *q*). For a suggested order, see Appendix B, page 86.

Framework Overview

Following are the basic steps on how to use this framework in your classroom. You will learn more about each step and its various components in Section 1. Repeat these steps for each new letter-sound.

Introduce sound(s) with Sound Cards

Using the appropriate Sound Card, introduce a new sound each morning to your entire class (see pages 88–122 for Sound Card reproducibles). First alone and then with your students, sing or chant the rhythmic chant that appears on the Sound Card and show your class the accompanying illustration. (The illustration visually demonstrates the sound.)

Card front

Card back

Letter: Rr Sound: /r/

Dog on a leash,
Trying to get away.
"No, doggie! No!
Stay, stay, stay!"
r . . . r . . . r

Select a letter-sound expert

Through a random drawing, select a student to "own" and become the "expert" for that letter.

Read emergent-level book

Read a pre-selected emergent-level book to your class (see Appendix B, page 86, for sample sentences and book list). This emergent reader will contain a sentence with a word that begins with the newly introduced letter-sound. Let the class know that the expert will eventually be in charge of reading this book independently to her/his peers. For the letter-sound /r/, for example, you might choose the emergent reader *In My Bed* by Rob Bacon. Later, this book will be placed on the Reading Wall for easy access.

Assign homework

Next, give the selected student her/his homework assignment. The assignment sheet includes the child's letter and sentence; it explains the process to parents and requires the student to return the next day ready and able to demonstrate her/his expertise (see Appendix J, page 166, for homework letter reproducible).

Students teach the class

The following morning the letter-sound expert will teach the entire class her/his letter-sound.

From a tub of prepared items, you will pull the pre-selected sentence for that expert. The morning of letter-sound instruction, place the pre-selected sentence on the chalkboard/whiteboard ledge. For example, a sample sentence for the letter-sound /r/ from *In My Bed* is: *There's room in my bed for my rabbit.* Write the letter *r* in red for the words ***room*** and ***rabbit***. The student tells the class what her/his letter is and what sound it makes, then shares an object brought from home that begins with that letter. The expert writes the letter (both in uppercase and lowercase) on the board. The student then reads the sentence and points to each word with correct one-to-one matching. S/he is now the class expert on that letter-sound, sentence, and book.

At the end of the day, or when your class is at recess, prepare the letter-sound expert's rectangle on the Reading Wall.

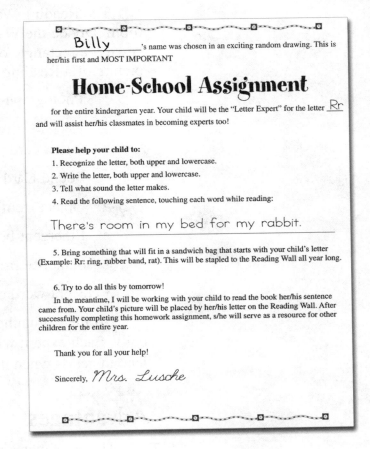

_____ Billy _____'s name was chosen in an exciting random drawing. This is her/his first and MOST IMPORTANT

Home-School Assignment

for the entire kindergarten year. Your child will be the "Letter Expert" for the letter __Rr__ and will assist her/his classmates in becoming experts too!

Please help your child to:
1. Recognize the letter, both upper and lowercase.
2. Write the letter, both upper and lowercase.
3. Tell what sound the letter makes.
4. Read the following sentence, touching each word while reading:

There's room in my bed for my rabbit.

5. Bring something that will fit in a sandwich bag that starts with your child's letter (Example: Rr: ring, rubber band, rat). This will be stapled to the Reading Wall all year long.

6. Try to do all this by tomorrow!
In the meantime, I will be working with your child to read the book her/his sentence came from. Your child's picture will be placed by her/his letter on the Reading Wall. After successfully completing this homework assignment, s/he will serve as a resource for other children for the entire year.

Thank you for all your help!

Sincerely, *Mrs. Lusche*

Reading Wall

The Reading Wall is a large visual display area in your room. Divide the Wall into individual rectangles. Each expert "owns" a rectangle on the Reading Wall (see page 23 for a picture of a Reading Wall), which displays:

- Photograph of the expert (taken on the first day of school)

- Letter card

- Sound Card

- Object from home that starts with the letter

- Emergent book

- Sentence from the book

- Sight word cards (add later in the year)

At the beginning of the year, review the Reading Wall daily. Each expert, with reading stick in hand, should lead the class when it's time to review her/his rectangle.

Advantages

The advantages to using this framework are many:

- This framework promotes learning for students of all abilities—while one student might be learning what sound *b* makes, another student might be noticing spelling patterns in the sentence in which the *b* is featured.

- This framework systematically promotes social and active learning and scaffolding by peers and teachers.

- Reading strategies, cueing systems, and assessments are automatically integrated into letter-sound study.

- Phonics instruction and assessment are directly linked to text students are working with each day in class—concepts are extracted from familiar text, examined, and returned to the text.

- This framework continually reinforces the connections between reading and writing: letter-sounds students decode while reading are encoded in writing; sight words used in reading can also be used in writing. The Reading Wall—a highly visible constant—is a valuable resource for both exercises!

- With 20 or more "letter-experts" in the classroom, students *own* the framework and instruction. As a community, they have built a letter-sound "co-op" to which they feel connected. You will find students depend on one another and hold each other accountable for individual and group progress.

- Fluency is encouraged with repeated reading of the same text. When decoding unknown text, children often fall into a staccato rhythm. As they become familiar with these sentences, they begin grouping words into phrases, and experience fluency!

So How Does It Work?

With adequate preparation before the start of the new school year, it takes very little planning to keep your letter-sound framework routine running smoothly once your students arrive. The students quickly come to understand the process and are eager to be in charge. For each successive year, you simply reorganize all the components and you're ready to begin again!

Be at Your Best: How to Prepare Before the School Year Begins

Preparing the Reading Wall

Before the school year begins, prepare an area large enough to accommodate 26 rectangular spaces (one for each letter of the alphabet). Each space should measure approximately 11" x 26" and be well defined. I use black rolls of art paper as the background and create the grid by stapling white strips onto the black. These spaces *must* be within student reach so students can easily retrieve their books and touch their sentences when reading. If you do not have enough wall space on which to create this grid, try securing materials to a portable bulletin board or the backs of student mailboxes.

Reading Wall

In the above photo, the rectangles form a grid, which measures three rectangles by nine rectangles. The configuration can change depending on room design, the most important requirement being that the entire class is able to see the Reading Wall as each expert leads the class in reading her/his sentence.

At this stage place only the letter cards (i.e., the uppercase/lowercase alphabet cards you normally post), in alphabetical order, on the rectangles. All other items are added as each student completes the homework assignment and assumes responsibility for her/his letter-sound. For those teachers who teach two sessions of kindergarten, or for those who share their rooms, the Reading Wall can be easily used for two groups of students; just add a second photograph and an additional object.

Collecting Supplies

Collect all the items listed below and place, in order, in a large tub (mine measures 10" x 16"). Store the tub in a convenient location, as you will need to access it each day you introduce a new letter-sound. Items include:

- Small container, holding the names of all students
- Sound Cards (reproducibles, Appendix C, pages 88–122)
- Emergent-level books (sample titles and sentences, Appendix B, pages 86–87)
- Sentence Strips (sample sentences, Appendix B, pages 86–87)
- Homework (reproducible letter to parents, Appendix J, page 166)
- Student photographs (taken of each student at the beginning of the year)

In another tub, make a copy of the expert's sentence. Cut this sentence into word segments. Put the cut-up sentence and a second copy of the expert's book in a Ziploc bag. Students use this bag at a center during Readers/Writers Workshop (see page 57 for more information on R/W Workshop).

Sound Cards

Make two copies of each Sound Card on heavy-stock paper. You will use one set to review sounds with your entire class; you will eventually use the other set for the Reading Wall (see page 34). Adhere the class set to the chalkboard using magnetic tape, or use them as flash cards.

1. What is the difference in emergent reader level designations? In other words, why is one book considered an early-emergent reader and another book an emergent reader?

The difference in level designations can sometimes be confusing, as different publishers have different gradient levels for their texts. One publisher, for example, might label texts as emergent, early, early fluent, and fluent, while another might use early emergent, upper emergent, early fluency, and fluency as designations. The books that fall within these categories are leveled with a numeric or letter designation.

When I refer to "emergent level" books in *No More Letter of the Week,* I mean those books that are small paperbacks, with very short texts. These are books that are specifically designed for our young budding readers (see page 26 for characteristics).

I place Cards on the chalkboard, adding one a day as each new expert is chosen. Together, the class reviews each sound as I point to the corresponding Sound Card. Students learn these picture-sounds easily, and they enjoy making the sounds as quickly as I can move the pointer from letter to letter.

The pictures on the Sound Cards have a strong kinesthetic component: the object in the picture "produces the sound," which you and the students act out. This is very different from most picture systems used to represent letters and sounds, in which the picture *starts* with the letter and sound (e.g., *p* is for *pear*). In this framework, for example, the /p/ Sound Card is represented by a boy spitting out seeds. When students see this picture, they make the /p/ sound by pretending to spit out seeds, thereby making a strong association between the physical action and the letter-sound. On the day you introduce this particular sound, have your students actually spit seeds into a trashcan. I guarantee they will *love* this part of the exercise!

Although you could use any picture-sound system for the Reading Wall, these "action sounds" are much more engaging for kindergartners. Having tried various types of picture systems, I have found the kinesthetic component outlined in this framework hastens learning, aids in retention (requiring less review), and produces many more smiles. In addition, these pictures do not require the auditory discrimination skills necessary to separate out beginning sounds from other sounds in the word. For example, if you use a picture of an elephant as a visual for the short /e/ sound, students might have difficulty discriminating between the short /e/ and the /e//l/ sounds in combination.

2. Is it important to have kindergartners experiment with books other than those from an emergent-level series? If so, in what capacity? What would students gain by working with trade books versus emergent-level books?

Some trade books share the same qualities as emergent readers—large print, patterns, short text cued by pictures, natural language, etc.—but they aren't easy to find, especially at the kindergarten level.

While there is no question trade books should play a significant role in the kindergarten classroom, with students being exposed to a wide variety of genres and styles during story time, activity time, shared reading, independent reading, library checkout, modeled writing, and even math, emergent readers are designed specifically with the beginning reader in mind. Because I can depend on emergent readers to best assist students in learning how to read, because emergent readers are the right size and weight for the Reading Wall, and because emergent readers are available in large quantities, I opt to use emergent readers over trade books for introducing letters and sounds.

3. If teachers do not have access to high-quality emergent-level titles, what are some alternatives?

First, it is important teachers make a solid effort to secure the books they need for their classrooms. Bottom line: children need books in order to learn to read, and good books help them learn to read faster by reinforcing essential literacy skills. If your district's budget is tight and you are not able to buy books with school funds, then

- write grants

- approach your PTCO

- ask parents to donate specific books in honor of their children's birthdays

- network with and borrow from teachers who do have substantial literature collections

If all else fails,

- photocopy reproducible books

- work with what you have

If you have only trade books in your classroom, then use them. Chances are you already understand your students' needs, which books are within their grasp, and which books they could learn to read independently. To check the reading levels of your trade books, you can access one of several sites available on the Internet, including www.titlewave.com. Check with your state department of education or your district literacy coordinator for other appropriate sites.

(continued on following page)

We usually progress through one, sometimes two, sounds a day.

Emergent-Level Books

Carefully select 26 emergent-level books. Each book should be engaging but also simple enough for the student to be able to eventually read independently. Rigby, Wright Group, Dominie Press, Sundance, and many other publishers offer a wide selection from which to choose. I have included a sample list of leveled book titles in Appendix B, pages 86–87. (See Resources, pages 172–173, for names and addresses of publishers who produce emergent readers.)

Emergent readers should include text that:

- tells an interesting story, with familiar concepts (e.g., doll/tree versus wheelbarrow/crane)

- mimics the natural language of the reader

- uses a consistent format (i.e., text is placed in the same position on each page)

- provides adequate spacing between words and lines

- contains a repetitive pattern, rhythm, and/or rhyme

- contains pictures that give a strong meaning cue

- contains high-frequency words

For the purposes of the Reading Wall, I recommend you avoid purchasing books with controlled vocabulary (e.g., The f_at c_at s_at on N_at's m_at.) or alliteration (e.g., The _big _bug _bit the _banana.), as such literature does not follow our natural language pattern; it is contrived and, therefore, distorts meaning. In addition, such texts focus emergent readers on visual cues only, making it particularly difficult, if not impossible, for students to utilize meaning and syntax clues so important to literacy development (Clay 1991). Good readers use a balance of cues to promote their fluency. Poor readers often stay at the visual, "sounding-out" level.

If possible, try to secure two copies of each book, the second copy of which students can use during Readers/Writers Workshop (see page 57 for more discussion on R/W Workshop).

Sentence Strips

After choosing the books, select a sentence from each that contains the appropriate letter (see Appendix B, pages 86–87, for sample books and sentences). As mentioned, start with those "high-utility" letters students will most frequently encounter in their reading—*r* and *s* versus *x* and *q*.

Type or write each sentence in black on sentence strips, with the featured letter(s) appearing in red. Select only letters at the beginning of words, not letters in the middle or at the end of words. For example, in the sentence *In came the horse* (from *The Pet Parade* by Andrea Butler), you would write the *h* in the word **h**orse in red, but not the *h* in the word *the*. As you did with the emergent books, place the sentence strips in the tub in the correct order. Students will use a second copy of each sentence, cut into word segments, as a center activity (see page 45).

Vowels are treated somewhat differently because two sounds will be on the Reading Wall for each vowel. Vowels are discussed in detail on pages 35–37.

If none of the trade books in your classroom is appropriate to teach your beginning readers and incorporate into the letter-sounds framework, you might also try one of the following:

• Select simple poems from a favorite children's poet—Shel Silverstein, Jack Prelutsky, Frank Lloyd Kramer—and have each student "own" a poem from which their particular sentence is excerpted. Post their poem on the Reading Wall.

• Write your own emergent readers! Hold a contest among teachers in your school or among upper-grade students. Set guidelines for them to create their very own books. Emergent readers should:

1. be 6–10 pages long

2. contain repetitive sentence patterns on each page (with just one or two word changes)

3. include "natural" language (text should *sound* like people *talk*)

4. include illustrations that fit within a 4" x 4" box (Provide a sheet on which the appropriate size box is printed. You will later cut out and paste this box into the emergent-level book.)

Provide each participant with an example of an emergent-level text, such as:

p. 1: I like the butter.

p. 2: I like the sugar.

p. 3: I like the milk.

p. 4: I like the eggs.

p. 5: I like the vanilla.

p. 6: But I like the cookies best!

Take a look at the Vowel Book reproducibles on pages 126–152 for additional examples and ideas on how text and illustrations should be formatted.

Homework Sheets

To start, simply make 21 copies of the homework sheet found in Appendix J, page 166 (one for each consonant), and write the consonant and its corresponding sentence in the designated spaces (see Appendix B, pages 86–87, for sample sentences; see pages 35–37 for more discussion on vowels). File the sheets according to the order sounds will be introduced. After a new letter-expert is chosen, you will simply add her/his name to the top of the homework sheet and give her/him the assignment.

If you have more than 21 students in a class, you have two options: you can assign "Buddy Experts" (two students who share the same letter-sound), or you can create a mini Reading Wall that displays the digraphs (*th*, *sh*, *ch*, *wh*) on four separate rectangles near the main Reading Wall (see Appendix B, pages 86–87, for sample books and sentences).

You're Ready to Begin!

Introducing a New Sound

Before selecting a new letter-sound expert, teach your students the following rhyme. Support the rhythm by alternating clapping your hands with tapping your thighs. This chant becomes a cue signaling the introduction of a new sound and, soon thereafter, the celebrated debut of a new expert!

City sounds, pretty sounds,

Nitty-gritty city sounds.

Listen for the sounds you need

To teach you how to learn to read.

Now, with the full attention of your class, introduce the new sound by singing or chanting the verse on the back of the

Sound Card. For the first Sound Card, /r/, the chant reads as follows:

> City sounds are all around,
> Words that you can say.
> Start with *r* and you will hear,
> It will sound this way . . .

If you are introducing a sound that is represented by more than one letter, say or sing the opening chant and then teach your class the following:

> City sounds are all around,
> Words that you can say.
> Start with *s* or start with *c*,
> And each will sound this way . . .

Now, with your students sing or chant the verse on the back of the Sound Card. For the first Sound Card, /r/, the chant reads as follows:

> Dog on a leash,
> Trying to get away.
> "No, doggie! No!
> Stay, stay, stay."
> *r . . . r . . . r*

Repeat the chant again, inviting your students to join in. Next, get down on your hands and knees and move around on the carpet, growling like angry dogs. When you're ready, signal students to stop making the sound. The action (to each sound) is the glue that makes these sounds and letters "stick." Encour age your class to act out each sound. From now on, whenever you hold up the Sound Card for the /r/ sound, your students should say "rrr," until you signal for them to stop.

Now, secure the /r/ Sound Card to the chalkboard using magnetic tape. If you are using the Sounds Cards as flash cards, simply introduce one sound at a time, and store flash cards in an easy-to-reach place.

We usually progress through one or two sounds a day so that by the end of four to eight weeks students have become familiar with all the sounds and many of the letters. The speed at which you introduce letter-sounds is not important, however, as students will *not* be waiting to read and write until all letters are introduced. Why? Skills are best taught "in action." Sounds and letters, therefore, should be taught in conjunction with reading, which is why it is important to introduce the high-utility letter-sounds first. Students can begin reading right away using book illustrations and patterned language, even when knowing only a portion of the sounds and letters they will eventually master. You will be amazed at how quickly students will learn their sounds with their Sound Cards. They can use each Sound Card (what they know) to bridge their knowledge to the symbol designations—e.g., *Aa*, *Bb*—what they don't know. The Reading Wall is close by for easy reference. In addition, when students are writing phonetically and need to record a sound, they will be able to locate the picture on a decoding chart and link it to the correct letter (see Appendix E, page 125, for Decoding Chart reproducible).

Note: When introducing a new letter-sound, it is imperative students say the correct sound. One common mistake is for beginning readers to add additional sounds to letter-sounds—for example, /puh/ for /p/. Proper tongue placement and mouth configuration are also important. For example, when making the /n/ sound, students should place their tongues behind their front teeth, at the roofs of their mouths.

City Sounds Big Book

If time permits, you might want to make a big book ("City Sounds") to introduce your sounds. It is a great organizational tool, keeping your Sound Cards in the correct order and enticing your students to review by reading the book.

> **Title on cover**
>
> City Sounds
>
> **Text for Title page**
>
> City sounds, pretty sounds,
>
> Nitty-gritty city sounds.
>
> Listen for the sounds you need
>
> To teach you how to learn to read.

The top portion of the left-hand page of each two-page spread should feature the chant specific to a particular letter-sound. For example:

> Dog on a leash,
>
> Trying to get away.
>
> "No, doggie! No!
>
> Stay, stay, stay."
>
> *rrr . . . rrr . . . rrr*

The bottom portion of each left-hand page should feature the following rhyme:

> City sounds are all around,
>
> Words that you can say.
>
> Start with *r* and you will hear,
>
> It will sound this way:
>
> *rrr . . . rrr . . . rrr*

Now, ask students to tell you words that begin with the sound /r/.

When the sound you want to teach is represented by two different letters (e.g., the /s/ sound for the letters *s* and *c*, the /k/ sound for the letters *k* and *c*), you would use the following rhyme:

City sounds are all around,

Words that you can say.

Start with *s* or start with *c*

And it will sound this way . . .

Place the enlarged version of each Sound Card on the right-hand page of each two-page spread.

And the Winner Is . . .: Selecting Letter-Sound Experts

Time for the first "random" drawing. Actually, the first expert (unlike those to follow) is not randomly chosen. I make sure that the first student whose name I "draw" is someone who will be a strong model for the experts that follow. So, with great enthusiasm, I pick a name from the name container, extend my congratulations to my new expert, and pull the appropriate book from the storage tub (for the letter *r*, I use *In My Bed* by Ron Bacon).

After you have read this book to the class, with the new expert at your side, ask students to guess which sentence has the /r/ sound (there may be more than one). Which sentence will go on the expert's rectangle? (Answer: *There's room in my bed for my rabbit*). Put the Sound Card for *Rr* on the board (or begin using your flash card collection).

Home(work)-School Connection

Give the Rr Expert a homework paper to work on that evening (see Appendix J, page 166, for the reproducible). Provided you have already written in the letter and the sentence, you will just need to fill in the expert's name. The note at the top of the homework assignment informs the parent that her/his child must return to school the next day able to:

- recognize the letter, both uppercase and lowercase

- write the letter on the board, both uppercase and lowercase

- tell the class what sound the letter makes

- touch each word while reading the sentence from the emergent-level book. (When the child performs this task, place the sentence strip on the chalkboard tray for the student to point to the words.)

- bring from home an object that begins with her/his assigned letter. (This object should be small enough to fit into a sandwich bag. I keep an X-ray on hand from a local veterinarian for the Xx Expert.)

Sample Reading Wall Rectangle

All the items are placed on the rectangle, as illustrated above. Staple the sentence strip (not the segmented sentence strip) onto the rectangle to create a pocket that will physically support the emergent reader.

At back-to-school night, I emphasize to parents the importance of this homework assignment. Inevitably, however, some students will return to school without having completed their task. When this occurs, I simply ask them to work on it another night, and I phone the parents to convey, once again, the importance of having their children practice reading the sentence and performing the related tasks. No matter what response you receive, it is important to remain positive and professional when interacting with those adults in your students' lives.

For students whose parents are unable to help them, for whatever reason, a teaching assistant, community volunteer, or upper-grade student can intervene. As students demonstrate their expertise, have them read their story and place the recommended items on the Reading Wall.

What About the Vowels?

It is necessary for emergent readers to make an early, clear distinction between vowels and consonants: When they are faced with decoding an unknown word but blending the sounds does not work, they need to be able to recognize which letter(s) is a vowel and at least two sounds it can make.

Eunice

Although many children can name the vowels—"a, e, i, o, u, and sometimes y"—it takes a more sophisticated level of understanding to be reading the word *hot* and know that *o* is the actual vowel and that, because *o* is a vowel, it makes at least two sounds. For example, if the text reads *The hot dog was good*, and the student reads *The hote . . . the hote. . .*, with exposure to vowel sounds, s/he should be able to recognize which letter(s) is a vowel and what sound it makes within the selected word. This provides an opportunity for the student to crosscheck meaning and graphophonic cueing systems. The student's thought process, for example, might be something like this: "*Hote* doesn't make sense. I know two different sounds for *o*, and I'm going to try the short sound: /h/ /o/ /t/—*hot dog*! Yes, that makes sense."

Save the Vowels for the VSP!

Because vowels are such a vital component in learning how to pronounce and understand words, I suggest you save the vowels for a vowel expert—a Very Special Person (VSP)—to teach.

The key is to make the vowels stand out. For instance, in my classroom, Eunice-the-Bunny is our vowel expert (a.k.a. the VSP). Eunice has been an integral member of my classroom for the past 16 years. She wears a kindergarten size six and changes clothes to reflect our unit of study. The students love her and know to look to her photographs on the Reading Wall for guidance in learning how to recognize their vowel letters and sounds. Your VSP can be anyone, however—your janitor, principal, classroom volunteer, photograph of your favorite author, or, like Eunice, a lovable stuffed animal.

Each vowel rectangle on the Reading Wall will eventually display:

- one photograph of your VSP

- two Sounds Cards (one for the long and one for the short vowel sounds)

- two objects starting with the long and the short vowel sounds

- one sentence strip, taken from the Vowel Book emergent reader (see Appendix B, pages 86–87, for sample Vowel Book sentences), on which you have written one sentence that contains words representing both vowels

- one reproducible emergent reader

When it is time to introduce a particular vowel, you can have your VSP model her/his expertise or take over the role yourself (consult Appendix B, pages 86–87, for the suggested letter-sound order). For instance, when reviewing the Wall, I tell students Eunice is shy, and therefore I am going to read the vowel rectangles the first few times. I then ask for a volunteer(s) to read one or more of Eunice's letters.

Frame the Sound Cards for vowels in the same bright color (e.g., neon red, orange, or green) to make them easily identifiable. As students view the Wall each day they see that the vowel rectangles each have two vowel Sound Cards and, therefore, understand each vowel makes at least two sounds. This knowledge is extremely useful when your readers begin reading and automatically know to try two sounds when decoding a difficult word with a vowel(s). You will be amazed at how quickly students learn the VSP's letter-sounds.

What About *Y*? I do not include the letter *y* in the vowel category. I tell students that the letter *y* sometimes acts like a vowel, but that they will be learning about that later. Most kindergartners do not reach the level at which they understand the role of *y* changes when it is added to the middle or end of a word. For those students who are ready to grasp this concept, teach them through a guided reading lesson later in the year.

Reading the Reading Wall

At the beginning of the year, I suggest you review the Reading Wall at a designated time each day. Reading the Wall before recess, for example, works well for my class. As Sound Cards begin to accumulate, review just a few rectangles (see page 41 for more discussion).

Student reading her sentence at the Reading Wall

Here's how a review session works:

- The student-expert who "owns" the rectangle gets the reading stick (pointer) and waits for everyone's attention.

- The expert leads the class in reading the letter, voicing the sound, naming the object in the bag, and reading the sentence.

The expert should model correct one-to-one correspondence. If s/he points to the wrong word when reading, prompt the reader to correct her/himself. In the following example, Lucy is touching the word *up* while saying the word *my*.

| *Lucy reads:* | "Mom, Billy used my red paint!" |
| *Actual sentence:* | Mom, Billy used up my red paint. |

In this scenario, I would ask Lucy to read the sentence again. If she repeats the same error, here's what I would say:

| *Teacher:* | "What letter would you expect to see at the beginning of the word *my*?" |
| *Lucy:* | "*m*." |

Teacher (touching the word up):	"Does that start with an *m*?
Lucy:	"No, that word starts with a *u*."
Teacher:	"Let's get your mouth ready (say the first sound) for that word. Now reread that sentence and check the first letter of each word you touch."
Lucy:	"Mom, Billy used u... up my red paint"
Teacher:	"You did it!"

When the class is reading from the Wall, they generally make few mistakes because the expert is in charge. We need mistakes, however, to reinforce and integrate other reading strategies and cueing systems. I have found the best teachable moments often present themselves when a student-expert is absent from the room and another student is chosen to read the expert's sentence, or when someone is chosen to be the vowel VSP and read the vowel sentences.

The Reading Wall Reinforces Essential Reading Strategies and Cueing Systems

The instructional opportunities are endless as students interact with their sentences on the Reading Wall. Teachers and students are able to systematically address, reinforce, and access:

1. Directionality (reading from left to right): For the most part, kindergartners do not experience problems with directionality. For those who do, however, the Reading Wall serves as a large visual on which they will learn, following a left-to-right pattern: students start by reading their letter on the far left, then they say the sound, and finally they look at the object in the bag. They continue with the left-to-right pattern as they begin to read the sentence. (See page 34 for an illustration of a Reading Wall rectangle.)

2. Sight Words or High-Frequency Words: These words appear often in the sentences you have selected from the emergent readers, and through constant exposure, students are able to learn them more easily. Children are always eager to see who "owns" the sight words that appear in the various sentences. (See "Sight Word Punch Cards," pages 47–49, for further discussion.)

3. One-to-One Correspondence: Practice, practice, practice. As the expert practices one-to-one correspondence, the readers must also match their voices to the expert's pointer as s/he points to each word.

4. Semantic (meaning) Cues: Teaching students how to identify semantic cues is a high priority, as students must always expect what they read to make sense. For example, when a student reads *Then Tommy got a tummy apple* instead of the exact text, *Then Tommy got a tummy ache* (from *Tommy's Tummy Ache* by Andrea Butler), prompt her/him to think about the story and about meaning: "Does that make sense? What's a *tummy apple*? Look at the picture. What does Tommy look like after he ate all those sweets? Let's reread."

5. Graphophonic (visual) Cues (searching for visual cues in text): Teach students to "get their mouths ready" for the initial sound of an unknown word. For example, when a student reads *Baby's spilling food* but the text reads *Baby's spilling peas* (from *Baby's Dinner* by Susan King), we refer back to the initial consonant of the word in question (*peas*). While pointing to the word *peas*, your conversation might sound something like this: "Does that look right? Could that word be *food*? What would you expect to see at the beginning of the word *food*? You're right, an *f*. Is that an *f* ? Oh, it's a *p*. Let's look at the picture. Make the /p/ sound and reread."

When students start reading word chunks (attaching sound to a group of letters instead of each individual letter: *-ing*, *-ed*, *-er*, *-and* [*hand*], *-all* [*ball*]), framing the chunks with your hands will help develop this strategy. Use the Reading Wall to reinforce instruction.

6. Syntax Cues (sentence structure): When trying to encourage children to listen to how our language sounds, we have the opportunity to ask them questions, to scaffold their thinking. For example, if the sentence on the Reading Wall states *The third one said, "Quick, let's run"* (from *Bang* by Graeme Gash), but the student reads *"The three one said, 'Quick, let's run,'"* you would say, "Is that the way we talk? Does that sound funny in your ear?"

7. Self-Monitoring and Cross-Checking Cues: Instead of pointing out an error, use general prompts such as: "Where was the tricky part?" or "Try that again," encouraging the student to take another look and check her/his reading. When a student recognizes that "something" doesn't match, help her/him through the process of checking one cueing system against another. If the student is unhappy with her/his response, ask her/him to consider the following questions: Does it make sense? Does it look right? Does it sound right?

Following is an example of a student using the cross-checking strategy (sentence excerpted from *Grandpa Snored* by Susan King):

Nathaniel:	"Grandma turned off the television—no! TV!"
Teacher:	"How did you know it was TV?"
Nathaniel:	"I saw the picture of the television." (semantic)
Teacher:	"But you said TV, not television."
Nathaniel:	"Television would have more letters than just two." (visual)
Teacher:	"Wow! I like the way you worked that out all by yourself."

The Reading Wall complements, supports, and reinforces the very skills you teach students for reading books and provides additional opportunities to teach those skills. When you teach skills using actual text, as opposed to isolating skills, you have an ever-expanding ceiling of teachable moments. Students are learning when they don't even know it!

As the number of completed rectangles increases (more than 15), on any given day, try just reading the top row, the bottom row, or just the letters with curves. On some days you might just practice a few letter-sounds, placing a paper clip on the rectangle you will start with the next day. Usually by midyear you will find it no longer necessary to read the Wall as a whole class, as students can now read and comprehend the sentences and engage the various sounds. However, the Wall will remain an important resource for the entire year.

You will discover that some children are not eager to give up the classroom ritual of reading the Wall and will choose to continue the exercise on their own free time, which you should encourage. Consider selecting a different student each day to read the Wall with her/his reading buddy (an upper-grade student or classroom volunteer) before they read books together. You will find the Reading Wall resurfaces in your modeled lessons, too, remaining an important resource throughout the year.

The Reading Wall helps bridge the known to the unknown; it is a shared resource constructed and owned by the students—a learning cooperative, if you will. And while you and the more advanced students in your class will serve as models and resources, each student becomes an expert on equal footing with her/his peers. From the Reading Wall, students begin to understand the purpose of and relationships among letter-sounds, words, and sentences.

Exceptional Punctuation

As per our usual morning routine, the students and I gathered in our group area for the opening sentence, which on this particular day included a comma. Lynn asked, "Why did you put that mark there?" I explained why we use commas and that they appear in many sentences. Immediately the students turned toward the Reading Wall to see which fortunate few had commas in their sentences. Those who did became the instant envy of their peers. And Alex became a real star when the kids saw that he owned the only sentence with quotation marks. While most children at this age do not fully comprehend the complexities of commas and quotation marks, they are beginning to build a foundation for that learning.

Notebooks

Once you and your class are settled into a good routine, provide each student with a three-ring binder large enough to accommodate 26 alphabet pages (see page 161 for reproducible notebook page) and any other additional pages, such as class songs and poems, you might want to include.

These notebooks:

- reinforce the importance of the illustration matching the text (reciprocity in reading).

- reinforce penmanship instruction and practice.

- provide a social, shared experience for reading familiar text.

- provide an opportunity for assessment through observation.

Each alphabet letter notebook page, organized in the order in which the letter-sound will be introduced, represents a different letter-sound and includes the following:

- the picture associated with the letter-sound (e.g., a flat tire for the letter-sound /s/)

- manuscript writing lines for letter-formation practice

Look at Lizzy touch the sky.

Student reviewing notebook page

- a space in which students can illustrate the appropriate sentence
- the letter-sound sentence, as it is written on the Reading Wall

Fill the notebooks with all the alphabet pages before you give them to students, and simply direct your class to a specific page for individual assignments.

After the student-expert has given a brief introduction to the notebook page, direct your class to practice forming their letters on the manuscript writing lines that appear at the top of the page by writing the uppercase version of the letter three times and the lowercase version of the same letter three times (for more discussion, see "The Importance of Penmanship," pages 44–45). Students should next illustrate a featured sentence. Work on one or two pages a week. The rate at which students finish their notebook pages is not important, as they do not need to be completed simultaneously with each letter-sound you introduce. Students may complete a page as part of a reading center or a whole-class activity. And while these notebooks stay at school during the school year, students may take the contents of their notebooks at the end of the year.

Class Poems and Songs

In our classroom, students also use the notebook as a place to store favorite class poems and songs and/or the chants that appear on the back of the Sound Cards. Should you choose to have students use their notebooks for this purpose, simply divide each notebook into sections using colored paper. Once students finish their penmanship and illustrations on the notebook page-of-the-day, they can review previous sentences, class poems, songs, and/or Sound Card rhymes.

Learning to Spell, Learning to Fly

One day four teachers from a distant school visited our classroom to observe. During our opening I asked for a student volunteer to write the word *fly* in the sentence on the white board. Freckly-faced Matthew came up and correctly spelled the word on the board. I asked Matthew how he knew how to spell *fly*, and he replied, "It's in Jessica's sentence: *An eagle can fly.*"

Illustrations

With your class, brainstorm illustration ideas for a particular sentence, stressing that student drawings must match the sentence.

Although it is important to allow students to use their own imaginations, you can help them get started by modeling how they might draw various objects mentioned in their sentences. For example, drawing a stick-figure horse or making kangaroos from a series of ovals provides students with a general idea on how objects are formed and makes it easier for them to get started.

This exercise helps kindergartners understand and apply the reverse of this concept when reading: in your notebooks, the words tell you what the picture should be about, while in reading, the picture tells you what the words will be about.

The Importance of Penmanship

Before students work on a notebook page, gather at the chalkboard for a short demonstration from the letter-expert on letter formation. The student-expert should remind her/his classmates to always start at the top and make sure the letter is sitting on the line.

With more emphasis being placed on reading expectations, I no longer dedicate whole-group classroom time to teaching penmanship. Instead, I depend on observation—while students are working on their notebook pages, for example—to assess and determine which students have weak fine-motor control and/or need more practice. I provide these students with additional practice and instruction time.

There are many options for helping students improve letter formation:

- Call on the class expert for the letter in question to teach a special "seminar" to a group of three or four students during playtime.

- Schedule teaching assistants, parent volunteers (in class and at home), and upper-grade students to help the children struggling with penmanship.

- Keep fun manipulatives on hand for students to use while practicing: salt trays, MagnaDoodle, shaving cream, your favorite pen, etc.

- Children who struggle with letter formation are often helped by auditory support. (See Appendix G, pages 153–156, for letter-formation directions.)

At the end of the year your class will be able to take home and read 26 beautifully illustrated sentences. Encourage students to teach their little brothers and sisters these sentences before they enter kindergarten. It's always nice for children (and teachers!) to have a head start.

Sentence Bags: A Center Activity

Utilizing Sentence Bags as a center activity allows students to actively study and manipulate familiar sentences with the use of cut-up sentence strips, while using a host of strategies discussed during Reading Wall time. The two primary benefits in using Sentence Bags are to encourage students to focus (i.e., to "get their mouths ready") on the first sound of the word and to hasten students' understanding of word boundaries and spacing. For example, some students know word boundaries (their name, a sight word), but they don't use spaces (*Kellysollthebln* for *Kelly saw the balloon*). Some students are beginning to grasp the idea of spacing, but they have not connected the spaces to actual word boundaries (I*sw amazgmin lls* for *I saw amazing animals*).

Sentence Bags

This Sentence Bag activity works well for all learning levels. The student just learning letters and sounds, for instance, will rely heavily on the letter books and her/his fellow students as models. On the other hand, the student already able to read will be able to focus on more advanced concepts such as spelling patterns, word order, and vocabulary choice. This center changes over time and can be adapted to meet different ability levels. For more discussion, turn to "The Evolving Read-and-Record Center" on pages 64–66.

Here's how Sentence Bags work:

As each sound is introduced, place a Ziploc bag in a storage tub in your literacy center or at a specially designated table. Label each bag with the letter it represents (e.g., *Rr*) and the number of cut-up sentence strip segments (e.g., *8*). Inside each bag include:

- the cut-up sentence for that letter (e.g., *There's / room / in / my / bed / for / my / rabbit.*)

- the book from which the sentence was taken (*In My Bed* by Ron Bacon)

- a letter book that shows different items starting with that letter (Dominie Letter Books, published by Dominie Press, Inc., work well for this exercise. See Resources, pages 171–173, for other recommended publishers.)

Introduce students to this center activity by modeling the following procedure:

- Read the selected books.

- Piece together the words written on the cut-up sentence strips so they create the correct sentence. Keep big spaces—approximately two finger widths—between each word.

- Check the order of the words by looking at the sentence in the book.

- Ask another student to read the sentence.

- Once students are successful at piecing sentences together, add another level by asking them to record sentences (see page 34 for sample sentence).

- Clean up the center by sorting the cut-up sentence strips into the appropriate letter-sound baggies. Then place these segments into their designated baggies (e.g., all the word strips with an *Ss* on the back belong in the *Ss* bag). Helpful hint: It helps to write the letter of the bag on the back of each word. Clean-up will go much faster.

Now that you have established the correct procedure, students may use this activity as a center, independently, or with their peers. (While I allow three or four students to work with Sentence Bags at a time, you might allow as many students to participate as there are bags.) Each student selects a bag and assembles her/his sentence, leaving big spaces, as indicated above, between each word. When you first introduce this activity, students may practice a sentence until they feel confident enough to select another. And whenever possible, leave time in your schedule to work with students one-on-one with this and other activities.

Sight Word Punch Cards

Have you ever noticed how excited students become when they recognize sight words in sentences? In observing emergent-reading behavior, I've witnessed how many times "landing" on a recognized sight word has kept students motivated. It is one thing for students to recognize and spell sight words isolated on their word lists and quite another for them to recognize these words when reading, or spell them correctly when writing. So what should they do? Practice, practice, practice! And while there exists a number of management systems for organizing these sight words—word rings, word banks, word journals—that work well if you have time to maintain them, for most busy classroom teachers, these systems are tedious and difficult to manage. To remedy the problem I designed low-maintenance, "teacher-free," Sight Word Punch Cards, which you can use to assess and reinforce sight-word study.

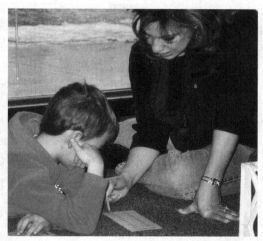

Volunteer working with student on his Punch Card words

In addition to being easy for the teacher to maintain, each student's personal Sight Word Punch Card set allows the student to feel a sense of ownership, and this spurs motivation. In past years I have found word walls to be ineffective with kindergartners because there is little interaction or ownership. The individual Punch Cards have the added benefit of providing a current assessment of what students know, and students can constantly interact with them, picking them up and bringing them as visually close as they need while writing.

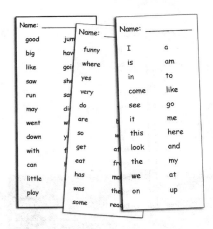

To create Punch Cards for your students, here's what to do:

For each student, photocopy one card at each level. (These are Dolch sight words; the lists become progressively more difficult with each successive level.) On heavy-stock paper, copy each level in a different color. Cut copies into 2" x 8" strips (see reproducible sight word lists, Appendix H, pages 157–159). Each student starts off with the Set 1 Sight Word List.

Once a week, you, a teacher assistant, or a volunteer should assess half the class on knowledge of their sight words (check the remainder of the class the following week). Punch holes next to those sight words students are able to say. Write the date of assessment on the back of each card. Once cards have been checked, students should place their cards behind the book on their rectangles on the Reading Wall. Now you and the student will know which words s/he should be held accountable for during reading/writing time. If you do not have an assistant teacher or a volunteer working in your room, check two students a day.

During writing time (see pages 60–61 for further discussion), have students take their Punch Cards from the Reading Wall and place them by their writing journals. When they are writing in their journal, they should write, in conventional spelling, any sight word that has been punched on their card. Students will be able to strengthen their retention of sight words through this reading and writing connection.

Once a student is comfortable working with a majority of the letter-sounds represented on the Reading Wall, send a letter home with a sight word card that has the first group of 22 words (see reproducible letter, Appendix J, page 167). Remember to store a copy of this list behind the book on that particular student's rectangle. When a student knows all the words on the first card, send the second card home and, as you did with the first, place this list behind her/his book on the Reading Wall. Follow the same procedure for the third set of words.

Most parents are excited and willing to help their children, and you will find most children, therefore, are excited to learn. By sending home this note, you emphasize the importance of this exercise with parents. Of course, as we all know, there will be some parents who are unable to work with their children. For these students, turn to peers, volunteers, and assistant teachers.

Students will not acquire these sight words at the same rate, nor will most students complete all three cards by the end of the school year (many will be working their way through the second or third card). If a student does learn all 66 words within the year, however, s/he will, without a formal list, continue to acquire sight words through independent reading.

Begin using Sight Word Punch Cards when you think your students are ready. I usually start after the first parent-teacher conference (12 weeks into the school year), so that I can explain the procedure to parents at our conference time. By then, the majority of my students know all of their sounds and most of their letters.

Student-to-Student Motivation

A teammate of mine came up with a great idea for encouraging students to quickly learn their sight words: A group of second-grade reading buddies works with my students every Friday. Before partners settle down to read, the "kindies" get their Punch Cards from the Reading Wall, and each second grader checks her/his partner's punched words. After this review, the second grader teaches her/his partner one or two new words. I leave the method of teaching up to the second graders. You would be surprised at how inventive and instructive their methods are! When second graders arrive the following Friday, they check to see if, during the previous week, I (or a volunteer) have punched a hole by the word(s) they taught their partners the week before. The second-grade students are genuinely excited about their partners' progress, and that excitement motivates our little ones!

Threading Literacy Throughout the Day

The framework for introducing letters and sounds is just one component supporting literacy in the classroom. The following section mentions other powerful opportunities that exist for students to interact with language.

Getting to Know You

The Photo Alphabet Book

Have the entire school get to know your class by making your students "visible" through a photo alphabet book. Create an alphabet book by binding 28 pages together (cover, alphabet letters, back cover; you could also include a title page). Alphabet letter pages should include a photograph featuring one or more students (individual students should be represented at least once), each in a different location within the school, and a sentence. For example, the *Nn* page might read: **N**annette and Bobby visit our **n**ice **n**urse. All words beginning with the letter *n* would have that first letter highlighted in a different color. The *Pp* page might read: Nicholas is **p**roud to be sitting at the **p**rincipal's desk.

Computer Connection

By photographing students in various spots around the school, you help them become familiar and more comfortable with people's faces and this new, oftentimes "scary," environment. In addition, students will enjoy taking this album home with them for an evening to show their families their new school and friends (they love to see their names in print!).

A close-up of Tyler's Photo Alphabet Book page

Take pages from a duplicate album and hang them up around the school. Now upper-grade students and teachers will recognize students by name while welcoming them, encouraging a sense of community.

Below is an example of my daily schedule to give you an idea of how I divide my day.

Kindergarten Schedule: Half-Day		
8:20 a.m.	**First bell rings**	• Meet-and-Greet
8:30	**Second bell rings**	• Opening: attendance, message, calendar, story
9:00	**Monday**	• Media Checkout
	Tuesday/Wednesday/ Thursday	• Readers/Writers Workshop
	Friday	• Reading Buddies
9:35	**Monday/Wednesday/ Friday** (alternating)	• Specials: art, music, gym, computers
	Tuesday/Thursday/ Friday (alternating)	• Math
10:15	**Recess**	
10:30	**Activity Time**: free-play, centers, work jobs	
11:00	**Closing**: Read big book	
11:20	**Dismissal**	

Making the Connection

Devon looked sad. He explained that his big brother had told him he was acting like a two-year-old and so he didn't want to walk to school with him. Devon needed to come to terms with his emotions by sharing them. Two other children then shared similar sibling stories, which led to a discussion about how Patricia Polacco had problems with her brother in *My Rotten Redheaded Older Brother*. Through this discussion we learned how most people have background knowledge about sibling relationships and rivalries. We talked about the connections we were making to each other and to books.

The Morning Matters

Morning Conversation

Oral language is the foundation of literacy, and it is important for every child to be given the chance, whether at home or at school, to openly and honestly communicate with his/her peers and with adults. In our fast-paced world, family dinners are on the decrease and television viewing is on the increase, so it is not surprising that our students' vocabularies are compromised. As teachers rush to meet curriculum objectives, it is important that we give students time to talk. The simplest—yet most powerful—act for you as the teacher is to make voice and eye contact with every student, giving each one the opportunity to communicate verbally (or, through expression, nonverbally) with you. When students arrive in the morning or while taking attendance, look at and speak directly to each student as you greet her/him by name, leaving the door open for conversation and further communication. It sounds so simple, but in the rush to accomplish "the agenda," we sometimes miss important messages children might want or need to share. And while you may not have time to extend every conversation, by making this direct connection, you are helping students feel like the important individuals they are. These moments make powerful backdrops for teaching.

Morning Sentence

Morning Sentence reinforces letter-sound relationships as they appear in writing—*in text*—and it is during this time when students learn a multitude of reading concepts and strategies: directionality; one-to-one correspondence; high-frequency words; and how to "get their mouths ready," segment and blend sounds in words, count syllables, and recognize letter chunks (e.g., *-ing*, *-er*, *-th*). They also learn about spacing, word boundaries, and punctuation. Because this activity offers so many elements to study, students can "plug in" at their own level of understanding.

Pick Me! Pick Me! In my classroom, students supply our morning sentences. If you choose to do the same, simply select a student from the sea of waving hands and ask her/him to share a sentence—any sentence—s/he likes. Record the sentence on the easel (at times I do all the writing; other times I ask students to write a portion). A typical sentence for the day might be: *My brother was sick and we had to go to the doctor last night*. Before writing the sentence, draw a line on the easel for every word you and/or the selected student will be writing. (I also utilize this procedure for their journal writing at the beginning of the year to scaffold the concept of spacing and word boundaries. As the year progresses, many students begin drawing their own lines and will discontinue this process when they no longer need that support.)

Fresh Language

Ben told us that last night he "taught his fingers how to snap" and tonight he was going to go home and "discover whistling." We all decided he should write about these experiences in his journal (because authors often take real-life experiences and write about them), and we complimented him on his "fresh" language—most people would just say, "I learned to snap my fingers" and "I'm going to learn to whistle." But not Ben.

Morning Sentence

Resources from Home

Our class had been talking about nocturnal animals since reading Audrey Penn's *The Kissing Hand*. Alyssa arrived in class the following day, excited to share a magazine article about a nocturnal bat. We compared Alyssa's article to our class copy of *Stellaluna*, Janell Cannon's fictional story about a bat searching for her self-identity. The class now had a personal model available to reinforce the concepts of fiction and nonfiction.

Elastic Words: When writing on the easel at the beginning of the year, stretch out all the words to make the sounds obvious, and ask students to tell you what letters you should write on the easel (for this activity, we use conventional spelling). Demonstrate by stretching a Slinky as you pronounce and "stretch" individual words. If a student responds incorrectly, gently praise any approximation and then elicit the correct response: "It's almost like a *b*, but it looks like this." "That makes sense to put a *k*, but what other letter might it be?" "You were so brave to try. Would you like to pick someone to help you with a second guess?" As the year progresses, students will be able to stretch most words themselves and will frequently write words correctly without your assistance.

Some words are more difficult than others, of course, and it is with these selections that we work as a real team, handing the dry-erase marker back and forth between teacher and student. For example, if a word is phonetically challenging (e.g., *through*), students might supply the sounds they know (*th* and *r*), while you supply the difficult segments (*-ough*). Explain to students that many words contain individual letter-sounds that are difficult, if not impossible, to sound out.

This Is a Letter. This Is a Word: Morning Sentence also provides an opportunity to discuss an important concept kindergartners and first graders often confuse: the differences between a letter, a word, and a sentence. After you have written the morning sentence, ask students to estimate the number of letters and/or number of words that appear in that sentence. If the student you call on tells you there are five letters in the sentence (or that there are twenty-five words), you know the student is confusing letters with words. The class then counts the actual number of letters and/or words; write these numbers on the whiteboard.

Address the difference between a letter and a word each day at the beginning of the year. When the majority of your class understands this concept, discontinue whole-group practice and work individually with those who need additional help. You might also try the assessment strategy in which a student uses two index cards like elevator doors (Clay 1993) while you say: "Open the doors until just one letter shows. Now close the doors. Open the doors until two letters show. Show me one word. Show me two words." Another strategy is to teach your students a song I wrote for my students to teach this difficult concept: "This is a letter, this is a word, this is a sentence, or so I've heard." While you're singing, ask a student to approach the easel and frame the letters, the words, and the entire sentence.

Morning Story

As part of our morning ritual, my class and I read a different story each day. The story may reflect a theme or author study, or it may simply serve as an excellent piece of literature that lends itself to one or more teaching points. Not only is this the perfect time to "hook" students on quality literature, it's the natural time to introduce and reinforce vocabulary, concepts, and thinking strategies related to reading, such as:

- author/illustrator
- dedication
- fiction/nonfiction
- genre
- rhyming
- characters/setting
- problem/solution
- schema (connections)
- questioning
- visualization
- retells (beginning/middle/end)
- prediction/inference

"I've Got an *ish* Word!"

In our class we call any word that is difficult to spell an "ish" word—whether or not it contains an "ish!" The term was actually coined years ago by a student while writing in his journal during Readers/Writers Workshop. As the parent volunteer was writing the conventional spelling under a word the student had written phonetically, he noticed there were many more letters than sounds. The student said, "That word is *ishy*; it doesn't make sense." From that point on his classmates began noticing "ish" words of their own. We've used "ish" to describe such vocabulary ever since.

Two Examples: Prediction and Inference

Prediction: When teaching prediction, for example, explain that predicting means making a good, informed/ educated guess: you guess what is going to happen next based on the clues you are given by the author and illustrator, in addition to what you already know (background knowledge/schema). Good readers do this all the time. Start out by modeling this strategy on several books, telling your students not only what predictions you make but *why* you made those predictions. Begin by modeling and slowly scaffold students to independence with this and other strategies.

Take a look at *The Napping House* by Audrey Wood. The reader can predict from the title and cover illustration that the book has something to do with sleeping and that the characters on the cover will, in all likelihood, appear in the book. The reader might also be able to predict that "something" will awaken the characters from their nice, long nap. Now it's time to dive in to find out.

Whether you pause in the middle of a book like *The Cow Who Wouldn't Come Down* (Paul Brett Johnson) to predict what will happen next and why, or predict the story of *Going to Sleep on the Farm* (Wendy Cheyette Lewison) based on only the illustrations, students will catch on quickly and will soon begin predicting stories themselves and explaining how they arrived at those predictions.

Inference: Now that you have a class of master predictors, talk with them about inference. The difference between predicting and inferring is that predictions can be confirmed by reading but inferences are never explicitly stated in the text. What can we infer about Chris Van Allsburg's "stranger" (*The Stranger*)? The author isn't going to tell us who his main character is or where he came from. We make inferences from the clues in the story. What can we infer from wordless picture books? Good readers infer things all the time. If children are dressed in shorts, we infer it is warm. If we see a shadow in an illustration, we infer it is sunny.

These concepts and strategies should be reinforced during guided reading and in students' writings and publications. The purpose of these discussions is to foster a *way of thinking* about text that promotes comprehension and generates a common language for shared literature. Together, you and your class are forming a foundation, the concepts and vocabulary of which can become a part of everyone's language as you explore the world of literature.

An excellent source for further information is *Reading with Meaning*: *Teaching Comprehension in Primary Grades* by Debbie Miller (Stenhouse Publishers, 2002).

Setting Up for Success with Readers/Writers Workshop

Readers/Writers Workshop functions differently in different classrooms. In my room, for example, it simply means that all students are engaged in some type of reading or writing activity while I spend the majority of my time with guided reading groups. Reading and writing permeate my daily program, but I set aside three days a week, 35 minutes a day, exclusively for whole-class reading/writing time—no assemblies, specialists, or other interruptions. I treasure this special time; it is the heart of my literacy program and the high point of my day—a time when the quiet hum lets me know that each child is completely focused on constructing meaning in reading and writing. On that perfect day, it wouldn't matter if I were in the room or not. Students know the system and they are in charge. And if I know I'm going to be absent for a day, I simply tell the substitute teacher to let the students show her/him how this literacy time works.

I strongly recommend that you recruit adult helpers to assist during Readers/Writers Workshop (see box on page 58). Should you have trouble soliciting volunteers, be creative:

- Use your school newspaper/letter to recruit parents.

- Approach community businesses and organizations interested in supporting education.

(continued on page 59)

Recruiting Adult Helpers

Make a strong attempt to recruit at least three parent helpers or community volunteers to assist during Readers/Writers Workshop (one volunteer per workshop per day, 35 minutes a workshop). At the very least, try to secure at least one volunteer who might be willing to help out two or three days a week. Back-to-school night is a perfect time to impress upon parents the importance of this extra help.

Once you know who will volunteer, make them feel comfortable and appreciated. During a volunteer training session, clearly explain your Readers/Writers Workshop routine and volunteers' responsibilities during this time, whether it be helping students through the writing process or, for those helpers unable to assist on a consistent basis, "dropping in" to work with students at reading centers.

At-Risk Students

If possible, schedule the special education teacher to work with any at-risk students right in your classroom during your workshop time. This teacher will become an integral part of your literacy routine. If s/he must work with students outside the room, try to have her/him schedule this time during Reading/Writing Workshop.

No Volunteers? Be Creative!

I am fortunate to be part of a team that shares a paid teaching assistant. (Initially the assistant's position was paid for by the PTCO, but it is now paid from the school budget.) We lobbied hard for this support when guided reading was introduced into the kindergarten classroom, and I am thankful for the assistance during our Readers/Writers Workshop.

- Write a grant or approach your parent/teacher organization to secure funds to assist in hiring an assistant.

- Approach local high schools and universities for student volunteers.

- Talk with your principal—could you "borrow" the school janitor, cook, or secretary for 35 minutes a week?

If you have exhausted all possibilities and are still unable to garner extra support, I suggest you postpone starting reading groups until students are comfortable with their responsibilities at Readers/Writers Workshop.

Let's Start at the Very Beginning: Reading and Writing

Before you introduce Readers/Writers Workshop, spend the first few weeks of the year convincing your students that they are ready.

Reading

A good way to start is by repeatedly sharing with them five or six books they are sure to enjoy. Big-book titles I have selected in the past include:

Mrs. Wishy-Washy (Joy Cowley)
Meanies (Joy Cowley)
Hairy Bear (Joy Cowley)
The Monster's Party (Tui T. Sutherland)
The Farm Concert (Joy Cowley)
In a Dark, Dark Wood (David Carter)

As a class, read and view these or other books of your choice until students become familiar with them. Place smaller versions of the big books along with familiar class songs and poems in tubs on tables around the room. Set aside 10 minutes a day for students to sit quietly at tables and read selections from their tub. We call this activity "Mumble Reading." Now students know they are readers.

Writing

To introduce the writing component of your workshop, as with reading, the entire class should be seated at tables and engaged in writing. This is an excellent opportunity to have your volunteer(s) observe your interactions with your students: "Wow! Tell me about that picture." "Read this to me." "You certainly know a lot of letters!" "You are so smart; how do you know *bike* starts with a *b*?" Start by giving students their very own journals. To create each journal, simply use plastic comb binding to bind together approximately 50 pieces of blank white paper, landscape format, with two or more lines at the bottom of each page. Make sure to leave plenty of space between lines. When students complete one journal, provide them with another.

Sample Journal Page

Students' first attempts at classroom writing will allow you to determine their ability levels, not to mention how they actually perceive writing. Some students will of course be shocked you would even ask them to write; some will draw pictures; some will scribble; some will produce nonsensical strings of letters, while others will be able to write words with accurate phonetic spellings; and there are those years a gifted student will guide you to a new understanding of the surprising level of competence they are able to attain.

During these initial writing experiences, you might consider providing students with writing prompts (although it is important for them not to depend on the teacher exclusively for ideas). Plastic objects (from phonics sorting games, for example), pictures, postcards, and a variety of environmental print would also work. Students can pick up a plastic object or look at the picture, tell you what it is, and stretch the word (segment sounds) to discover the sounds. For instance, a student might pick up the plastic dog figure and stretch the word *dog*: d . . . o . . . g. If they produce the sound but don't know the letter, they can use the Decoding Chart (see Appendix E, page 125, for reproducible) to find the needed letter(s) independently.

Praise students for any and all attempts at writing, keeping in mind that for many this may be their first time putting pencil to paper in order to communicate. The more they practice and the more you praise them, the more comfortable students will become with the writing process and with their initial approximations. Soon they will come to understand they are all writers.

Readers/Writers Workshop Rotation

After approximately two weeks of the above activities you are ready to begin rotations in Readers/Writers Workshop. This time frame, however, is flexible in order to accommodate the overall ability level of your class.

Half your class should be at the writing tables (located by the Reading Wall), preferably with a teaching assistant or parent volunteer. The other half of the class is divided among three reading centers, with three or four students at each center. If a student writes one day, the next day s/he is a reader, and vice versa. Post a rotating chart somewhere in the classroom that tells students where they should be each day.

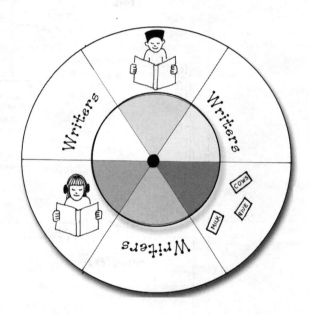

Rotating Chart

The room arrangement on the following page allows for an organized separation of groups.

After experimenting with many systems that required students moving back and forth between centers in short intervals of time, I have opted for a system that offers more in-depth centers and less transitioning, allowing students to stay at one center for the entire workshop period. Each center either offers a variety of activities or changes throughout the year. With this change, our classroom became a more peaceful and productive place.

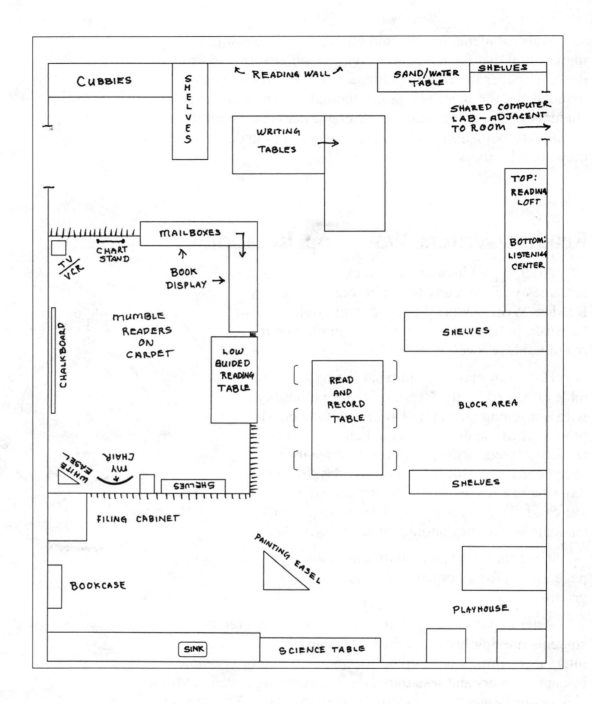

Effective room arrangement

Reading Centers

Students not involved at the writing tables engage in activities at one of three reading centers.

Mumble Center

Designate a carpeted space for your Mumble Center. What is a Mumble Center? Because kindergartners should not be expected to read silently, as few of them have developed an inner reading voice, the Mumble Center provides a place where they can quietly read self-selected stories out loud. Individually or with a group of two to four peers, students can select a guided reading book(s)—books they will recognize from their guided reading time—from one of the guided reading tubs (see pages 66–71 for more on guided reading). Once they have read at least two guided reading books, they can move on to reading class charts, songs, poems, big books, and other trade books, all of which are stored in the Mumble Center area. "Mumble Readers" remain on the big carpet until the workshop period is over.

Mumble Center

Listening Center

The Listening Center welcomes two to four students with cozy beanbags, a warm light, and a good story, all nestled under our Reading Loft. In this center students listen to a recorded book and then move to the top of the loft to review a collection of alphabet books. Later in the year, the alphabet book tub is replaced with an overhead projector. This projector is on the bottom level of the loft near the tape recorder. Students love using magnetic letters on the overhead to write and project sight words onto the wall. A folder of transparencies is available, along with favorite class poems, charts, and songs. And don't forget a finger pointer!

Listening Center

The Evolving Read-and-Record Center

The Read-and-Record Center evolves throughout the year and is actually a designated table where students can experiment with a variety of activities.

Each day before students start work in this center, they should grab the center supply tub, which contains a multitude of relevant items. When the focus of the center changes, so do the materials in the tub. This center can easily change to match your current objectives. The following activities may be easily adapted to meet the special needs of individual students.

Write Your Name: Students will enjoy starting off the year by practicing writing their names in different colors and with different utensils. The supply tub for this center can contain crayons, chalk, markers, glitter pens, and vibrating pens. Another activity students enjoy is piecing together name puzzles. Name puzzles are easy to make: simply write students' names on individual pieces of tag board, decorate (or have students decorate), and cut out in puzzle-piece shapes. You might also consider purchasing pre-cut blank puzzle pieces, available through many teacher-supply stores or catalogs. To store, place puzzle pieces in plastic bags and then put them in the center tub. Depending on your class, you might choose to do some beginning consonant sorts (e.g., place all the pictures in this pile that start with a *p*; put all the pictures in this pile that start with an *r*).

Build a Sentence: After students have spent the first few weeks of school practicing writing their names or working through initial consonant activities, change the focus of the center to sentence construction. The tub for this center should contain the same sentence bags as were discussed on pages 45–47. Students construct sentences according to these same directions. Once students

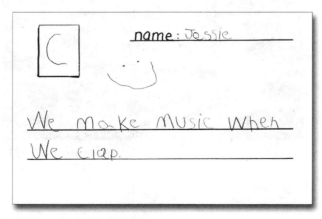

Recorded Sentence

master piecing sentences together, ask them to record their constructions on paper (see Appendix I, page 162, for reproducible).

Rhyming Picture Match and Record: During the last part of the year change the center to Rhyming Picture Match and Record. In this center, students work with 10 sets of rhyming picture cards (two sets of 10; 20 cards in all) depicting items that rhyme: cat/hat, door/four, girl/squirrel, etc. On the front of each card is the picture, and on the back of each card is the picture name. Students match rhyming pictures together by looking at pictures first. They then turn the pictures over and record the correct words from the backs onto a reproducible recording sheet (see Appendix I, page 164, for reproducible).

Rhyming Picture Match and Record

Sight Word Read, Sort, and Record: When students are ready to move on to another activity, change the center to a Sight Word Read, Sort, and Record. Simply take the 2-, 3-, and 4-letter sight words that appear on Punch Cards (see pages 47–49 for previous discussion; see pages 157–159 for reproducible lists) and write them on 3" x 5" index cards. Place these cards in the center tub. One student deals the cards out equally among the children. Each student, in turn, reads one of her/his cards and places it in the correct pile. Thus the index cards are sorted into three different groups: sight words with two letters, sight words with three letters, and sight words with four letters. When it's time to offer a more challenging activity, add the recording component. Students select words from each group (two, three, or four letters) to record on paper. Once the cards are sorted, students record some of the sight words (see Appendix I, page 165, for reproducible) in the correct place.

Rhyming Words

Sight Word Read and Sort

For review purposes, students should place recorded sheets in a designated area located near your chair. At the conclusion of R/W Workshop, you may use these papers as a tool from which to make a couple of quick teaching points (or reinforce expectations and accountability) before the author(s) of the day shares her/his work.

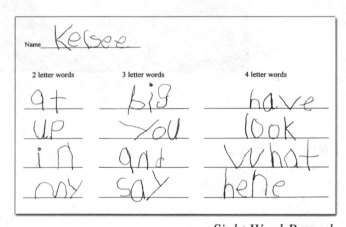

Sight Word Record

Guided Reading with Kindergartners

Begin structuring and meeting with reading groups once your students understand the Readers/Writers Workshop routine and are able to work at centers independently or with their peers.

In my classroom, reading instruction is based on guided reading principles and procedures and works as follows:

- At the beginning of the year, I form reading groups based on students' abilities to identify letters. As the year progresses, groups become fluid and change often.

- I meet with a group of two to four students at a specially designated guided reading table for 10 to 15 minutes at a time. The table at which we meet is low to the ground (approximately two feet high), so we actually sit on the floor. The guided reading books are stored at one end of the table.

Guided Reading

- We start each lesson by reading the book with which we concluded the previous lesson. During this time, students read quietly to themselves. I listen to each student and note her/his reading behaviors (What strategies are they using [praise]? What strategies do they need to use [prompt]? Are they monitoring their own reading? Are they using a balance of cueing systems?) I might interrupt an individual student's reading for discussion, or I might wait to share a teaching point with the entire group at the end of the lesson.

- Next, I introduce a new book, highlighting what the story is about (picture focus), discussing what background knowledge students might bring to this particular story, pointing out one or more words or concepts that might prove challenging, and possibly identifying repeated language patterns.

- Using their "soft voices," the students read the new story quietly to themselves. I listen, intervening when needed and jotting down errors, all the while deciding which teaching point(s) (strategy or cueing system) I will focus on after students have finished the book. My teaching points usually include one or two of the following:

  * Group procedure and behavioral expectations: Did students remember to bring their group's book tub to guided reading? Are students reading independently,

using their soft voices? Once a student has finished reading the book, does s/he start rereading until the rest of the group has finished?

* One-to-one correspondence: Are students matching their voice to print? (Are they touching the word while they are saying the word?) Ask: "Does that match?" Do they need to remove their fingers from the book because the text is easy?

* Meaning/semantic cues: Did students look at the picture(s)? Did they think about the story? Ask: "Did that make sense?" "Let's reread the sentence."

* Searching for structure/syntax cues: Ask: "Can we say the word that way?" "Does it sound funny in our ears?"

* Searching for visual/graphic cues: Does what they're saying match how the word is written on the page? Are they "getting their mouths ready" to say a word (the first sound of the word in question)? Ask: "Does it look right?" "Could that word be . . . ?" "What letter would you expect that word to start with?"

* Cross-checking the cueing systems: Are students checking more than one cueing system at a time? Ask: "Does it make sense and look right?" "Does it sound right and look right?" Prompt students to check the picture, get their mouths ready, and go back to the beginning of the sentence. Post a visual aid (see Appendix I, page 163, for reproducible) by the Guided Reading Center to help students with this cross-checking strategy.

* Sight words: Are they able to read words that they know on their Sight Word Punch Cards? Can they make analogies between words? You might say: "If you know the word *day*, then you know the word *way*. You wrote *he* in your journal, and this word is like the word *he*. You're right, the word is *we*."

* As groups advance, concentrate on identifying chunks in words (e.g, -*ing* in *thing*) and blending sounds.

- Once students finish their reading, first respond to the content of the story, always making meaning the priority. Next, highlight one or two teaching points. For example, if your teaching point focuses on students "getting their mouths ready," talk about an example or two in which a student(s) used this strategy successfully:

Text: See the door.

Student starts to read: "See the d . . . d . . . d (then checks the picture) door."

Now use one or more examples in which a student(s) did not use the strategy correctly:

Text: See the window.

*Student looks at the picture
then reads the text:*   "See the curtain."

While it is important to praise the student for looking at the picture, remind the entire group that they must also "get their mouths ready." They need to say the sound of the first letter of the word they are touching *and* look at the picture (if they are having difficulties reading the word) before attempting to read the word. Groups return to their assigned literacy center after each lesson.

During guided reading time make use of a large white-board or small, individual whiteboards. While you may not incorporate a writing component into each lesson, you might find this a good time to practice reading and spelling sight words or identifying common chunks found in words.

It is important to note that guided reading isn't part of any rotation schedule. I am free to shorten, lengthen, or postpone my groups. This gives me the freedom to respond to any emergencies or special needs that might arise (tears, visitors, exciting writing, etc.) without disrupting the workshop atmosphere.

Guided Reading: Good First Teaching for All Children by Irene C. Fountas and Gay Su Pinnell and *Guided Reading: A Practical Approach for Teachers* by the Wright Group provide in-depth information.

Guided Reading with Struggling Readers: Alphabet Books

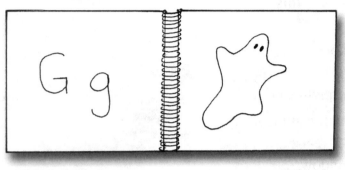

Alphabet Book

In each year's class there are typically three or four students who at the end of the first month of school are still able to identify only ten or fewer letters/letter-sounds. These students need more reading support. I usually work with a total of six different guided reading groups, and meet with two or three groups a day. I make sure I hold a guided reading session with each group, especially those who struggle, every other workshop day (once or twice a week). It is important that these students begin reading books (like the other students) and not be limited to isolated letter-work only. Knowing all your letters is *not* a prerequisite to reading books.

To introduce and reinforce our guided reading lessons, I give each struggling reader her/his very own personalized Alphabet Book. They are colorful, instructive, and easy to make.

To create, simply bind together twenty-six 8 ½" x 5 ½" blank pages (landscape format). Make a master with each letter of the alphabet either typed or written (uppercase and lowercase) on the left-hand page. Next, have students select pictures they would like to glue onto the right-hand side of each letter page of their individual Alphabet Books. I keep a file of pictures I have collected for each letter-sound. In the past, I have purchased alphabet stickers from Resources for Reading (see Resources, page 173, for contact information). You don't have to purchase stickers, as you might choose to duplicate pictures from any number of resources—magazines, environmental print materials, or old books. Have your students find them for you during free time.

At the beginning of your lesson have students glue on one or two pictures to the appropriate letter page (each vowel page should have two pictures, one for the long sound and one for the short sound) and quietly read the pages they have already completed in their Alphabet Book. (Do this prior to reading the text the group concluded their previous guided reading lesson with.) To introduce a new letter, start out by saying the letter name, then making each individual letter-sound by running your fingers down the inside spiral, and finally naming the alphabet picture. Students create books at their own speed. Whereas letter-sounds on the Reading Wall are introduced within the first eight weeks or so of school, your struggling students may take the entire year to create their Alphabet Books.

Now you can review the previous lesson's text and introduce a new story.

The Writing Center: Guided Writing

Once students have seen you model writing Morning Message, and have experimented with writing as a class, they are ready to engage in guided writing with the support of an adult. Keep in mind that the "with the support of an adult" component is vital to scaffolding students to becoming successful, independent writers. Too often, we, as teachers, model how to do something and then expect the class to work independently, without any support, and this inevitably leads to frustration for many students. Students will move more efficiently through the writing process and feel more secure in their writing attempts with their teacher or an adult helper present to guide and encourage.

While approximately half your class works on Reading Center activities, the other half should be writing in their journals at designated Writing-Center tables. If at all possible, try to have two or more helpers to assist students one-on-one as needed.

Page 72 shows a sample conversation you or an adult helper might have with a student at the beginning of the year to help the student verbalize, and eventually write, her/his story in her/his writing journal.

This conversation continues through the word *tornado*, with the student writing as many letter-sounds as s/he is able to hear. When the student is finished, write the correct spelling under the inventive spelling:

Trndo
Tornado

Un-post the Post-it Note

I used to write conventional spellings for students on Post-it Notes—and not directly on their papers—as I was afraid I would discourage these young writers with this infringement. Over the years, however, I have found that if you congratulate students for attempting to spell a word, they won't mind you writing directly on their work. In fact, placing the correct spelling next to their invented spelling, as seen at left in the Tornado example, allows students to recognize the gaps in their spellings.

Adult:	"Tell me about your picture."
Student:	"It's about a tornado that blew up all the houses and trees."
Adult:	"Wow! That sounds exciting, but scary. I hope this didn't really happen to someone you know. I'll put a line here for the word *tornado*. What sounds do you hear in the word t-o-r-n-a-d-o?" (If the student can't stretch the word, the adult should accentuate sounds by slowly stretching out the word.)
Student:	"/t/"
Adult:	"Okay. Write a *t*. What other sounds do you hear: *t-o-r-*"
Student:	"/r/"
Adult:	"Oh! You're so smart. Let's try to identify another sound with a letter: *t-o-r-n-*."
Student:	"/n/ like the *airplane*. What does an *n* look like?"
Adult:	"Check your decoding chart. Show me the airplane."
Student:	"Here it is." (Student writes the letter *n.*)

As students progress in their writing, help them write longer sentences and stories, encouraging them to stretch words on their own and offering help only when they are not able to perform the task themselves. For those writers who continue to write sentences without leaving spaces between each word, draw one line for each word in the sentence (short lines for short words, long lines for long words), until the student eventually understands the convention.

Adult helpers must continually filter their conversations through this basic premise: Praise students for what they know and gently nudge them to the next step without automatically providing them with the correct answer.

Celebrate (and Educate) with Author's Chair

At the close of Readers/Writers Workshop, it's time to celebrate, motivate, and provide further literacy instruction by using your students' own writing as a backdrop for your teaching objectives. Allow featured authors (two different students per day) to sit in a special Author's Chair and share their writing—whether it's the word *balloon* or an entire story about a balloon.

This "teachable moments" time allows students the opportunity to talk through their thought processes, and it offers everyone the chance to reinforce concepts and spur discussion on such topics as:

- pictures: Do pictures help tell the story? Could the author add more relevant detail?

- content/idea: Is the story interesting to listen to? Does it make you want to know more? Is there any fresh (creative) language?

- sentences: Are sentences clear, dynamic, and easy to read? What type of punctuation is used?

- details: What could the author add to her/his story?

- sounds: What letter-sounds do students hear in individual words?

- spacing: Has the author left a space between each word?

- prediction/inference: What can the class predict or infer from the author's writing?

Computer Connection

Computer programs such as Waterford reinforce letter-sounds, phonemic awareness, and print concepts. Students—especially those who need repetitive practice—will enjoy the engaging visual and auditory components as they work their way through the various learning levels.

Publishing

At the beginning of the year, publish your students' early attempts at writing. If a student writes *b* for *balloon* in her/his writing journal, for example, type the word *balloon* onto a single sheet of paper and ask the writer to illustrate her/his writing. Make two copies, one for the student to take home and one for you to file in the student's published-works folder. The writing journals are incredibly valuable as an assessment tool and are fun to share at conferences. Everyone—teacher, parents, students—will be able to clearly see the exciting growth that takes place in these journal pages. For those students who choose to publish their work, I suggest you publish at least twice a month. As they gain confidence in their abilities, students will start writing sentences and, eventually, stories, which they can publish in book form. Whether a student has published two books or ten by the end of the year, your class will be sure to enjoy the satisfaction of seeing its work displayed in your classroom library.

Students reading their published books

When publishing your students' first books, require only that they have a topic they can talk about for at least three sentences (two or three days' work). It might be as simple as *I went camping. I found a rock. I came home*. That's fine. As the year progresses, however, require more from your writers, helping them to revise their work and make it stronger. For example, when a student turns in her/his journal, in which they have written a story they would like to publish, return it to them with a pointed, content-related question—"Amanda, what did you do when your sister got hurt?" Discuss with students how they can expand their stories, problems, and solutions within their writing, dialogue, punctuation, or any number of additional elements they are tackling in this activity. You and your volunteers will help scaffold students in this revision process.

After printing the children's text, provide simple covers that excite and entice the reader. Create shape books, window-flip books that open up to expose school photographs, or flip books. The easiest and most common technique, of course, is to take a rectangular book and cut just the top edge to match a particular story element (e.g., mountain peaks, tree tops, bunny ears).

Laminate and store these colorful books in your classroom library for the entire year, and encourage students to read their own titles and their classmates' books during Readers/Writers Workshop and playtime. Use class writings to reinforce concepts during whole-class lessons or one-on-one instruction.

Make a video of individual students reading their books. Students can check out the video to share with their parents. Many of my less-motivated students began producing books just because they wanted to be on TV!

Model and Share Your Own Writing

I am fortunate to have had the opportunity to publish an emergent reader, and I enjoy sharing with my class the thrill of publication. I show students the torn yellow sheet of paper on which I wrote the original version (all 43 words); they hear about my son's basketball game and how I jotted down notes when the players were on the sidelines; I show them the letter of acceptance I received in the mail and the rough sketches the illustrator sent for my approval; they see the revisions the editors made to my text; and finally I show students the published product, *The Inside Story.* They cannot believe that it is *my* book.

Whether or not you have published a book professionally, it is important that you share with your students your writing in its various stages. This makes writing very real to them. For example, write and illustrate your own big books and store them in your classroom library right alongside the professionally published books. Encourage students to do the same. As a class you can share the frustrations and excitement related to this creative process.

Students will also appreciate learning from and about professional authors like Cynthia Rylant or Tomie dePaola. What are their passions? Frustrations? How do they search for new ideas? These are real people who, along with you, can make a real and purposeful difference in your students' lives. Be a model by exploring with students your own relationship with writing.

End the Day with Shared Big Books

Reading a book is the perfect way to begin and end the day with your kindergartners, who come to expect a high level of social involvement during this group time. I suggest you use the big-book format for this activity, as big books are large and therefore more viewable. In addition, most big books actively engage students with their repetitive refrains and large, expressive pictures: students enjoy "churning" their bodies to the "wishy-washy" refrain in *Mrs. Wishy-Washy*, and they can't wait to play the horn, fly, dance, and sing in *The Monster's Party*. Children bounce excitedly, their hands in the air, hoping to be chosen to come up to the book and point out special letters and words. Kindergartners inevitably gain confidence in their reading abilities by repeating ("reading") the popular refrains, and they will want to revisit big books again and again.

The Parent-Homework Connection

Take-Home Bags

During back-to-school night, ask for one or more crafty volunteers to sew together Take-Home Bags. Each bag should be approximately six inches wide by seven inches tall and contain a plastic name pocket on the outside in which you can feature each student's name. At the end of the year, collect the bags and remove the names from the plastic sleeves. Now they're ready to use for next year's class!

Ziploc bags work well, too, but the home-made bags are festive and, therefore, more motivating.

Student reading with classroom volunteer

Three mornings a week, while I am involved with the class in our morning-opening routine, an adult volunteer or teaching assistant comes in for about 30 minutes to read with children one-on-one (so if you have a class of 21 students, the volunteer/teaching assistant would read individually with 7 students for roughly 4 or 5 minutes per visit). The adult selects an emergent-level book to read with the student; the student takes this same book home to read with her/his parents along with a "completed-assignment" slip (see Appendix J, page 168, for reproducible) for her/his parents to sign. Once students have completed a title, they bring in their Take-Home Bag (with book and slip), the adult selects a new title, and the process is repeated. When the entire assignment slip is filled, ask adult helpers to place it on your desk. You can now file each student's slip in her/his folder and use it as a visual during parent-teacher conferences.

I keep a collection of emergent books that are filed by level in boxes (Velveeta Cheese boxes work well for dividing leveled books) on a bookcase by the teaching assistant/volunteer's workstation. Most kindergartners start on the simplest level and move up when the books become too easy. I check their levels periodically to see if they correspond to their guided reading levels. If I note students are reading too far above or too far below their levels, I will ask the assistant/volunteer to select books closer to students' guided reading levels.

Should you choose to do this same school-to-home activity, be sure to file the completed-assignment slips in your student files. At parent conferences, these visible records demonstrate to parents the integral relationship between their involvement and their child's success at school. This exercise also provides you with one more trained volunteer out in the school community who understands the reading process and just how hard *you* are working.

Parent-Student Homework Assignments

I assign parents their first parent-child homework assignment at our back-to-school night. I then change the homework assignment at the first and second parent-teacher conferences.

Assignment: Word Stretch

Request that parents begin stretching words—any words—with their children for about five minutes each night for the first twelve or so weeks of school. I do not require completed-assignment slips for this assignment, but I do impress on parents how important their assistance is and how easily I—"the all-knowing, expert teacher," I say with a smile—will be able to identify those students who have received this extra practice. Parents have the option to document word-stretches, but I do not require that they pass these in.

After you have demonstrated to parents how to stretch words (see sample dialogue on the next page) so their children hear all relevant sounds, provide them with the following instructions:

- Stretch one word per night.

- Ask your child what sounds s/he hears.

- Write down the letters your child tells you. If s/he misses sounds or doesn't know the letter, just write the letter for her/him. The word will be spelled correctly in "book spelling" (my kindergartners call conventional spelling "book spelling"—how a word appears in a book).

For those words that do not have a simple sound-to-letter correlation, tell parents to acknowledge the letters of the sounds the child hears (e.g., *l-a-f* for *laugh*), praising her/him for her/his approximations, before writing down the correct spelling. For example, the parent should write *l* then *a*, if the child knew those two letters, but when the child says *f*, the parent should respond: "You're right, it sounds like the letter *f*, but we write it this way: *l-a-u-g-h*." Model the following dialogue with parents:

Child: "Let's write *sky*."

Parent: "Okay, what do you hear at the beginning." (If the child doesn't respond, parent says /s/.)

Child: "*s*"

Parent: "You're right!" (Parent writes an *s*.)

Child: "I hear an *i*, too."

Parent: "Let's stretch it to see what the *next* letter is." (Parent makes the following sounds: /ssskkk/.)

Child: "*k*!"

Parent: "You're right!" (Parent writes *sk*.)

Child: "*i*!"

Parent: "It sounds just like an *i*, but it's a *y*." (Parent writes *sky*.)

At the first conference of the year, show parents the first and last pages of their child's Writing Journal. They will be astounded by the contrast of these two pages, as most students start out by drawing on their journal pages, but by the end are writing sentences with two or three letters per word. Seeing this difference really helps parents feel a part of this progress—which, you can assure them, they most certainly are—and they are eager to provide their support. I tell parents that this one-on-one attention by someone students love cannot be easily duplicated in the classroom.

Assignment: Write a Sentence

At the first conference ask parents to start a second 12-week assignment with their sons and daughters: Write a Sentence. Here's how this works:

- Give parents a letter outlining the assignment.

- Provide students with a booklet (12 sheets of lined 8 ½" x 11" paper stapled together) labeled "My Homework." To give these booklets a more personal touch, students can decorate their covers.

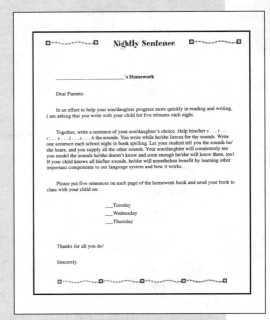

- Each school night parents and students should take out this booklet and write a simple sentence, one repeated from an earlier conversation, so that by the end of the week they have written five sentences on one page.

- Children should focus on what sounds they hear in each word as their parents write the words down in the booklet. (Children provide the letters they know; parents provide the rest.)

- Assign each student a day of the week on which to turn in her/his homework booklet (in our classroom Tuesdays, Wednesdays, and Thursdays are sentence days). Have students deposit their homework booklet at a designated area, such as a homework tub. Once you have read each booklet, take a minute or two to respond with a quick note—*Wow!* or *Me too!* or *Sounds like fun!*—something to let them know you did indeed read their sentences. Next, place a stamp next to the last written sentence so parents know their children turned in their homework booklet. Finally, return booklets to student mailboxes or cubbies. Color a square on the "Returned Homework" graph for each student who returns her/his homework.

The "Returned Homework" Graph: The Benefits of Accountability

Create a large graph labeled "Returned Homework." As students turn in their homework on their assigned day, color in a square of the graph under the appropriate day of the week. If a student forgets her/his sentence booklet, send home a reminder note. Color in the appropriate square when the student does bring in the assignment. Graph homework for 12 weeks.

Let parents know how important it is for them to work with their children on assignments and to turn these assignments in on time. Impress upon them not only how valuable this parent-child time is, but how the in-class graphing lesson depends on the timely completion of these tasks. Be sure to send home a note to parents when assignments are late.

Inevitably, there is also some peer pressure by each child's group (groups are determined by which day students have been assigned to turn in their homework) to add a level to the graph. By holding parents accountable, you increase the chances they will take the time to work with their children (which is my goal).

Assignment: Write a Sentence

For the final 12 weeks of the year, ask students and parents to continue with the previous assignment, as you will continue to respond to, stamp, and send home their sentences. I suggest, however, you discontinue the late notes and the graphing.

This homework assignment repeatedly reinforces what students know and models for them what they don't yet know. And like other components of the kindergarten program, it is a broad enough activity to benefit all kindergartners— Jason may be learning the /g/ sound while Jeremy is starting to recognize the *-ight* pattern in words. Perhaps the most valuable aspect of this assignment is the opportunity for students to work with and learn from the people they love best—their parents.

This is also a very important assignment for parents. Not only are they active participants in their children's education—responsible in large part for growth and success—they are also developing a much better understanding of the challenges and successes involved in their child's learning process. Parents get excited when they see their daughter or son getting stronger. And this, of course, makes the students themselves more motivated and excited.

And Finally . . .

Make frequent connections among student-experts, teaching points, and the Reading Wall throughout the school day:

"Cassy, ask Rachel how to make that letter."

"Does anyone have that word on their rectangle?"

"Remember when we were reading the Wall and Caitlin said . . . ."

"Who has the /ch/ sound in their sentence on the Reading Wall?"

"Some expert has a rhyming title on their book. Who is it?"

When implementing this method of introducing letters and sounds, I offer some final thoughts.

Let the power of ownership reinforce your students' confidence. The confidence a child feels by actually knowing how to independently read the emergent books is a natural reinforcement—reading has its own rewards. Publishing your own writing also reinforces learning. Stickers, promises, and other extrinsic motivators work very well short-term, but they do little to develop independent, self-motivated learners. Allow students the satisfaction of earning your respect.

Parents as partners. The more parents understand your program and your commitment to your students, the better your chances are to enlist their support. If a parent does anything for the class, show your appreciation by making an announcement, for example, on your weekly voice-mail message: "Thank you, Mrs. Buckner, Andy's mom, for coming in to help with the video camera. Andy sure was smiling a lot in that video!" Parents will appreciate the recognition.

Maintain the balance. Establish high expectations through developmentally appropriate practices by finding the balance between meeting academic requirements and creating an appropriate learning environment for your young learners: Are your students choosing to read and write? Are they approaching their tasks with eagerness? Are they laughing, thinking, and interacting with the text and illustrations? Are they utilizing the student-experts and the Reading Wall? Successful teachers are the ones who find a way to engage their students in literacy with the same enthusiasm they bring to the water table or the building blocks. That takes talent, knowledge, planning, and close observation of each and every student. Watch your students closely. They will inform your teaching.

Appendices

Appendix A Systems and Strategies
- Cueing Systems and Strategies
- Comprehension Strategies

Appendix B Sample Letter-Sound Sentences

Appendix C Reproducible Sound Cards

Appendix D Sounds in Action/Suggested Actions

Appendix E Reproducible Decoding Chart

Appendix F Reproducible Vowel Books

Appendix G Directions for Letter Formation

Appendix H Punch Cards
- Set 1 Sight Word List
- Set 2 Sight Word List
- Set 3 Sight Word List

Appendix I Additional Reproducibles
- Notebook Page Directions and Samples
- Build-a-Sentence
- Reading Procedure
- These Words Rhyme!
- 2-, 3-, and 4-Letter Words

Appendix J Reproducible Letters to Parents
- Home-School Assignment
- Sight Word Support
- Completed Assignment Sheet
- Nightly Sentence

Cueing Systems

Cues are sources of information that can be located within the text and accessed by the reader. There are three major cueing systems:

- **Semantic (meaning):** what the story is about and how it connects with the reader's background knowledge. *Does it make sense?*

- **Syntactic (sentence structure):** how our language works; how words come together in an expected structure. *Can we say it that way?*

- **Visual (graphophonics):** letter-sound association. *Does it look right?*

Strategies

Strategies are operations or behaviors the reader applies to text. Important strategies that researchers such as Clay (1993) identify include:

Directionality:

- tracking from left to right
- making a return sweep to the left of the next line
- reading from the top to the bottom of the page
- reading the left page before the right page

One-to-One Correspondence: touching each word as it is read

Locating Known Words: recognizing sight words in text

Locating Unknown Words

Self-Monitoring: checking oneself using available information and strategies and then cross-checking by using more than one cue or strategy at the same time

Searching for Cues: actively checking the picture and rereading for meaning, listening for correct syntax, and searching for visual cues ("getting your mouth ready")

Self-Correcting: self-monitoring and cross-checking so the reader is able to identify and fix mistakes s/he discovers

Comprehension Strategies for Readers:
The Thinking Processes We Use in the Act of Reading

Adapted from Dole, Duffy, Roehler, and Pearson (1991) and Benson (2002)

1. Identifying What Is Important in Text

- relevant versus irrelevant information
- main ideas/critical ideas, themes
- key words, signal words
- titles, headings, graphs, charts, captions, table of contents, etc.

2. Drawing Inferences

- predicting, testing, confirming
- drawing conclusions
- inferring ideas
- knowing what is needed to obtain information in text from schema

3. Using Prior Knowledge (Schema)

- activating experience/prior knowledge/schema

4. Asking Questions

- asking self-generated questions before, during, and after reading
- considering how questions affect comprehension

5. Monitoring Comprehension

- identifying when you know and understand what you have read; when what you have read makes sense
- understanding when you do not know or understand what you have read; when what you have read does not make sense
- knowing what you need to know

6. Fix-Up Strategies/Repairing Our Reading

- what to do when meaning breaks down

7. Synthesizing Information

- summary

8. Visualizing

- the pictures in your head while reading/your movie for the text

Letter	Sound	Sentence	Book	Author	Level	Publisher/Series
Rr	/r/	There's **r**oom in my bed for my **r**abbit.	In My Bed	Ron Bacon	RR®	
Ee	/ē/ /e/	"You will not **e**at my **e**ggs!" yelled Mama Turtle.	Eggs for Breakfast	Pat Lusche	3	*
Ss	/s/	Look at Lizzy touch the **s**ky.	Dizzy Lizzy	Lucy Lawrence	8	****
Nn	/n/	He is going down the stairs.	The Skier	Beverley Randell and Jenny Giles	2	****
Tt	/t/	See my **n**ose.	All of Me	Andrea Butler	2	*
Oo	/o/ /ō/	Grandma **t**urned off the **TV**.	Grandpa Snored	Susan King	9	**
Kk	/k/	Come and look at the **t**urtle.	Big Sea Animals	multiple	2	******
Ii	/ī/ / /ī/	Mom put honey **o**n Molly's **o**atmeal.	Not Oatmeal!	Pat Lusche	3 PL	**
Pp	/p/	When I **k**ick, I **k**ick.	When I Play	Andrea Butler	3	*
Dd	/d/	There **i**s **i**ce cream on his hair.	Ice Cream	Pat Lusche	3 PL	
Ll	/l/	Baby's spilling **p**eas.	Baby's Dinner	Susan King	7	**
Mm	/m/	"My home is here," said the **p**ig.	My Home	June Melser	2	WGSB
Zz	/z/	This **d**ress has spots.	What Has Spots?	Jackie Goodyear	2	**
Aa	/a/ /ā/	They put on lipstick.	Dressing Up	Beverley Randell and Jenny Giles	3	****
Hh	/h/	Cows give **m**ilk.	On the Farm	Ron Bacon	5	*
Bb	/b/	I saw a kangaroo feeding people in the **z**oo.	I Saw a Dinosaur	Joy Cowley	11	**
Vv	/v/	Come and see the **z**ebra.	At the Zoo	Beverley Randell and Jenny Giles	2	****
Gg	/g/	Will you smile **a**t the **a**pe?	Please Smile	Pat Lusche	2 PL	*
Jj	/j/	In came the **h**orse.	The Pet Parade	Andrea Butler	4	*
Ww	/w/	**B**uffy chased a **b**all.	Buffy	Tui Simpson	7	**
Yy	/y/	I had **v**egetables.	The Well-Fed Bear	Lucy Lawrence	2	*
Qq	/kw/	I **g**o to school in a **v**an.	The Way I Go to School	multiple	2	**
Xx	/ks/	Some things **j**ingle and **j**angle.	Noises	Beverley Randell	2	WGWB
		Number 10 gets in **f**ront.	The Race	Beverley Randell	7	**
Uu	/ū/ /u/	Green **f**ootprints on baby doll's head.	Green Footprints	Connie Kehoe	7	**
Ff	/f/	Mom, Billy **u**sed **u**p my red paint and my blue paint.	Billy's Picture	Pat Lusche	3 PL	
		Then Tommy **g**ot a tummy ache.	Tommy's Tummy Ache	Andrea Butler	3	*
		What does a **w**itch **w**ant?	The Present	Jenny Hessell	7	**
		Here comes the **w**inner!	The Go-Carts	Beverley Randell and Jenny Giles	2	****
		Dear Santa, thank **y**ou for the kite.	Dear Santa	David Drew	2	**
		The third one said, "**Qu**ick, let's run."	Bang	Graeme Gash	9	***
		Quack, **qu**ack. Here we come!	Time for Dinner	Beverley Randell and Jenny Giles	2	**
		Here I am in the **X**-ray room.	My Accident	Jenny Giles	4	*****
Cc	/k/	We make music when we **cl**ap.	We Make Music	Robyn Connery	5	**
Digraphs						
wh	/wh/	"**Wh**ere's the egg cup?" asked the witch.	Where's the Egg Cup	Joy Cowley	2	WGWB
ch	/ch/	Here is a table and a **ch**air.	Here Is . . .	Beryl Smith	2	***
th	/th/	**Th**e books go here.	In Our Classroom	multiple	1	DPCR
sh	/sh/	**Sh**e is up on the wall.	Climbing	Sharlaine Cairns	2	****

Publisher/Series Key

* Rigby, Literacy 2000, Stage 1

** Rigby, Literacy 2000, Stage 2

*** Rigby, Literacy 2000, Stage 3

**** Rigby, PM Collection, PM Starters One

***** Rigby, PM Collection, PM Starters Two

****** Rigby, PM Plus, Starters One

******* Rigby, PM Plus, Starters Two

WGWB: Wright Group, Windmill Books

WGSB: Wright Group, Story Box®

DPCR: Dominie Press, Carousel Readers, Red Level Set

• RR®: Reading Recovery® Levels

• PL Vowel Book Levels: The author of the Vowel Books has, to the best of her ability, determined the levels equivalent to Reading Recovery levels. Please note the Vowel Books have not been leveled by a Reading Recovery specialist.

Sample sentences have been excerpted from the appropriate publishers. Each publisher's contact information may be found in the Resources section on pages 171–173.

Sound Cards

City Sounds

Written by Pat Lusche
Adapted by Frank Lloyd Kramer

Illustrations by Phyllis Pittet

Illustrations for letter-sounds /o/, /d/, and /u/
by Macie Durr Adapted by S. Dunholter

Sing or chant this verse to let students know it is time to learn a new sound:

City sounds, pretty sounds,
Nitty-gritty city sounds.
Listen for the sounds you need
To teach you how to learn to read.

City sounds are all around,
Words that you can say.
Start with *r* and you will hear,
It will sound this way: (say/sing the sound)

Replace the chant above with the following rhyme when two different letters make the same sound (e.g., /s/ for *s* and *c*). Sing or chant the following:

City sounds are all around,
Words that you can say.
Start with *s* or start with *c*,
And it will sound this way: (say/sing the sound)

Where's the Cc Sound Card? A Cc Sound Card is not included, as the purpose of this sound system is to introduce *sounds* (and their corresponding letter[s]). Since the letter *c* makes the /s/ sound and the /k/ sound, discuss the letter *c* when you introduce the letters *s* and *k*. Adapt the introductory rhyme as shown above. When discussing *k*, simply insert the line: "Start with *k* or start with *c*. . . ."

For the Cc rectangle on the Reading Wall, you might either assign the Ss Expert and the Kk Expert to work together, or, if you have enough students, you might assign a student to work on this rectangle by her/himself.

Big Book Adaptation: Enlarge Sound Cards and rhymes and bind into a big book. Place Sound Cards on the right-hand side and rhymes on the left-hand side. Use for instruction and/or store in your classroom library for students to "check out." (See page 31 for more discussion.)

Photocopying Directions: The rhyme for each letter-sound appears on the back of each illustration. Simply set the photocopier to print double-sided. Use a paper cutter to cut cards to the appropriate size.

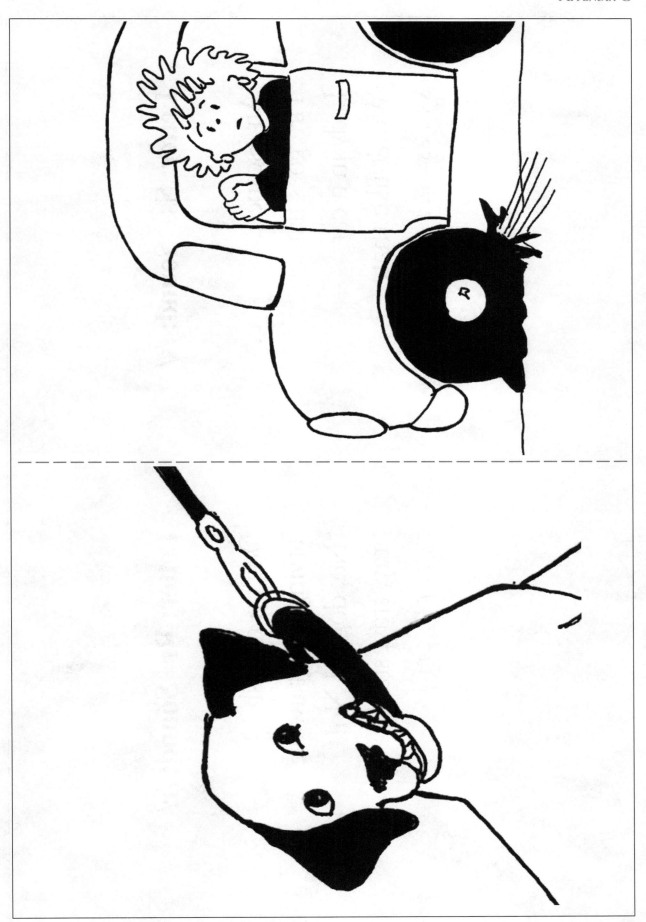

89

Letter: Ss   Sound: /s/

Air escapes;
Tire goes flat.
Lady in a car
Won't like that.

s . . . s . . . s

Letter: Rr   Sound: /r/

Dog on a leash,
Trying to get away.
"No, doggie! No!
Stay, stay, stay!"

r . . . r . . . r

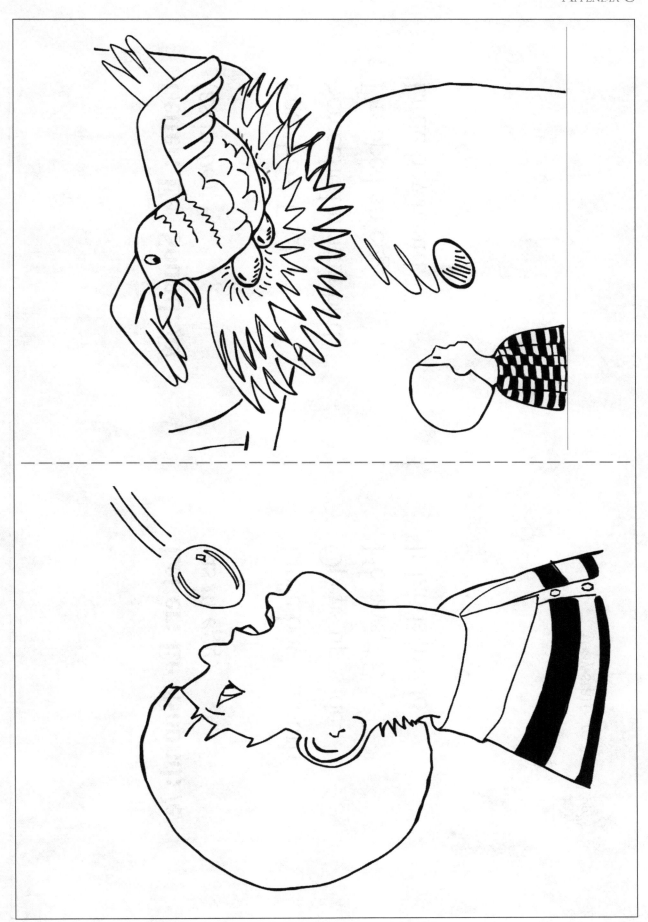

91

Letter: Ee Sound: /ē/

(as in *be*)

Eee! Eee! Eee!
Screeched mama bird.
Dropped an egg,
Little boy heard.

e . . . e . . . e

Letter: Ee Sound: /e/

(as in *egg*)

Little boy's mouth
Opens up wide.
He says, "E . . ."
It lands inside.

e . . . e . . . e

(boy starts to say "Egg")

Crystal Springs Books (2003)
Reproducible

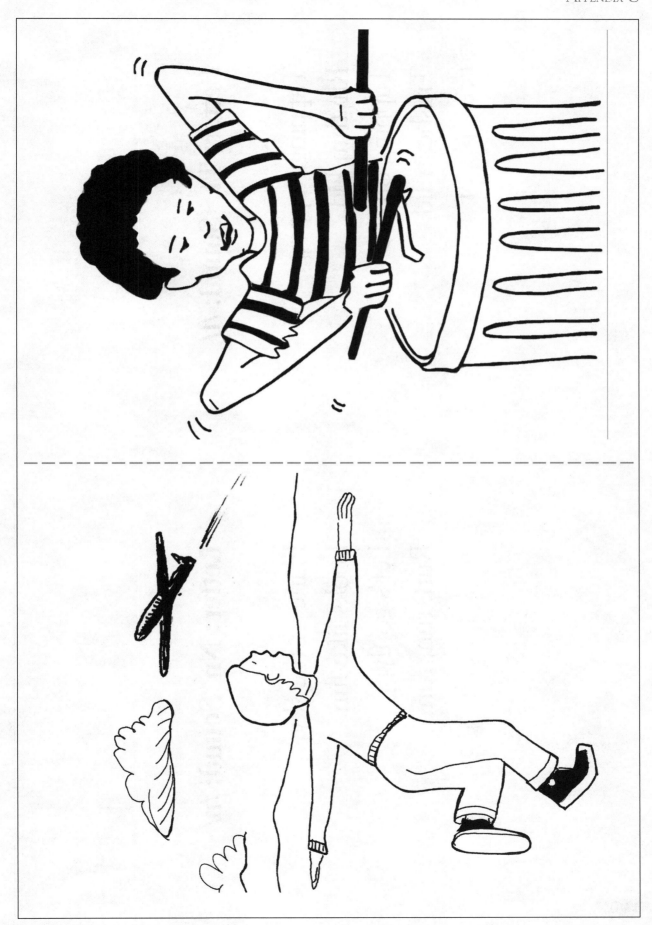

Letter: Tt Sound: /t/

Tapping, tapping,

Rhythm kid.

Tapping on the

Trashcan lid.

t . . . t . . . t

Letter: Nn Sound: /n/

Plane in the sky;

Looks like fun.

Let's go fly;

Run, run, run.

n . . . n . . . n

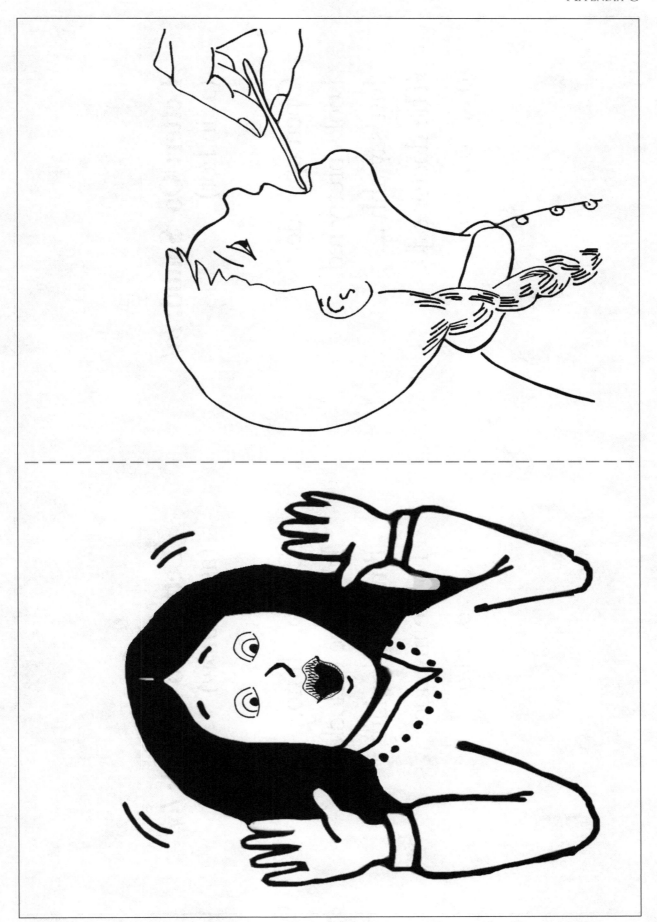

95

Reproducible

Letter: Oo Sound: /o/
(as in *hot*)

Open up wide.
Looks pretty red.
Just say ahh.....
The doctor said.

o ... o ... o

Letter: Oo Sound: /ō/
(as in *know*)

Oh no, oh no,
It's three o'clock.
I'm late, I'm late
To see my doc.

o ... o ... o

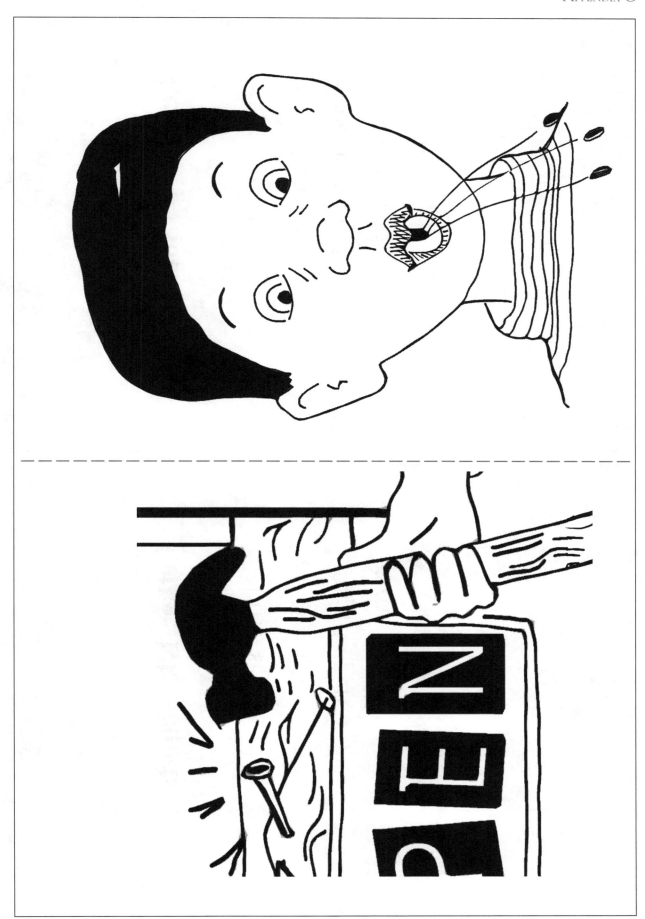

97 **Reproducible**

Letter: Pp Sound: /p/

Spit them out,
If you please.
You should not
be eating seeds.

p . . . p . . . p

Letter: Kk Sound: /k/

Nail this sign
to the door.
Time to open
Up the store.

k . . . k . . . k

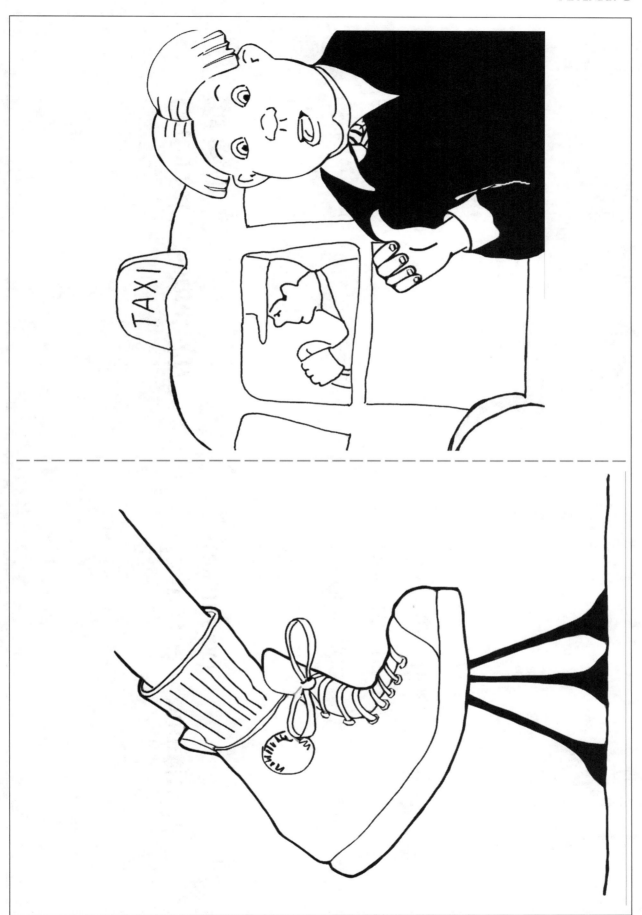

99 Crystal Springs Books (2003) **Reproducible**

Letter: Ii   Sound: /ī/
(as in *I*)

I, I, I
Get to ride
In this taxi.
Hop inside!

i . . . i . . . i

- -

Letter: Ii   Sound: /i/
(as in *tick*)

What a mess.
Gooey, goo.
Sticking to my
Favorite shoe.

i . . . i . . . i

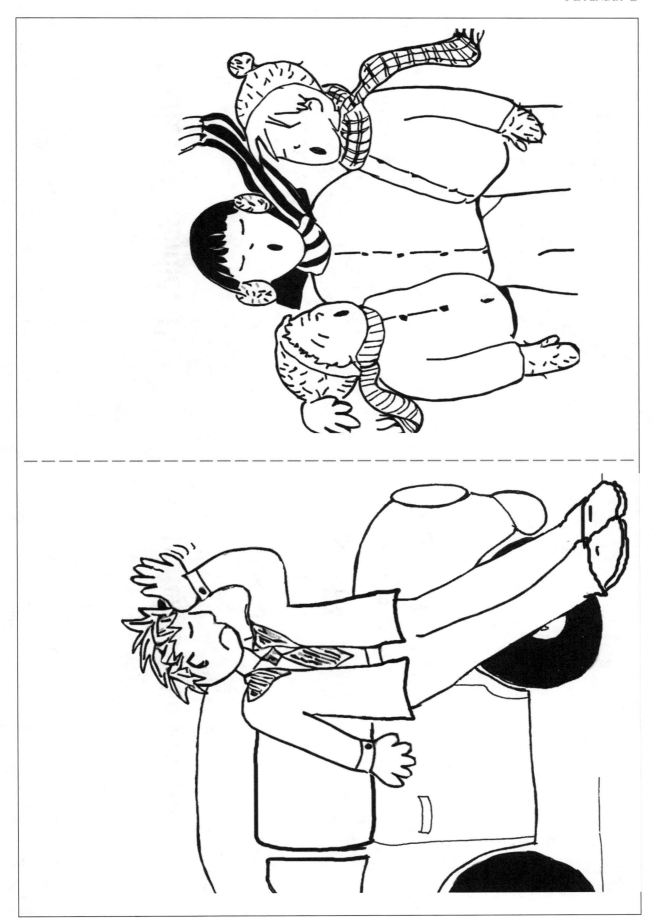

Letter: Ll   Sound: /l/

l . . . l . . . l,
Children sing.
l . . . l . . . l,
Sing that thing:
l . . . l . . . l

(sing the /l/ sound)

Letter: Dd   Sound: /d/

Locked my keys
in the car.
Not too smart!
Won't go far.
d . . . d . . . d

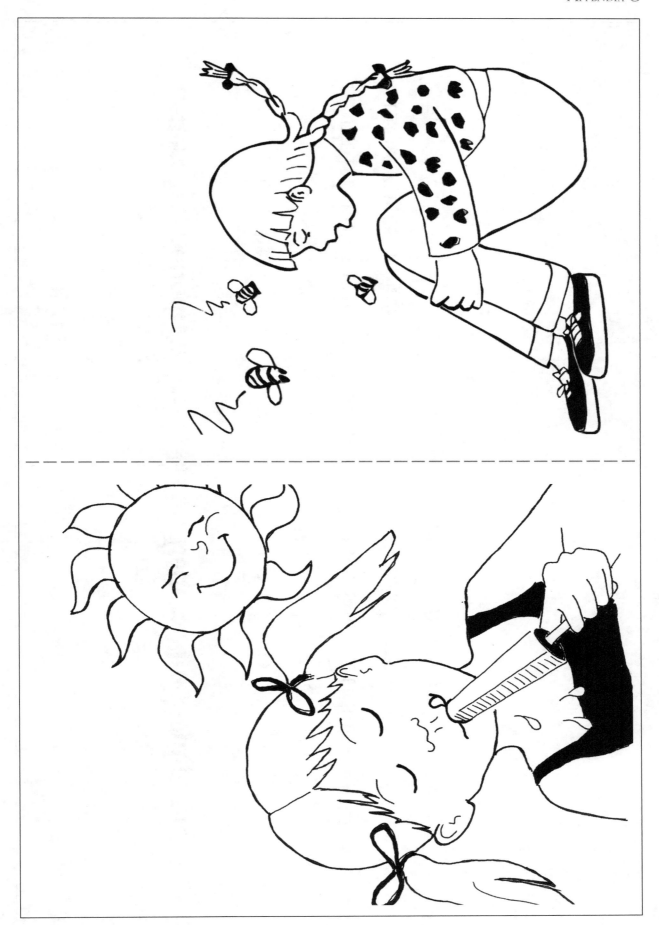

103 Crystal Springs Books (2003) **Reproducible**

Letter: Zz Sound: /z/

Bees, bees, bees,

Please, please, please

Don't land on my

Knees, knees, knees.

z . . . z . . . z

Letter: Mm Sound: /m/

Popsicle cold,

Popsicle sweet,

Hot summer day.

Popsicle treat.

m . . . m . . . m

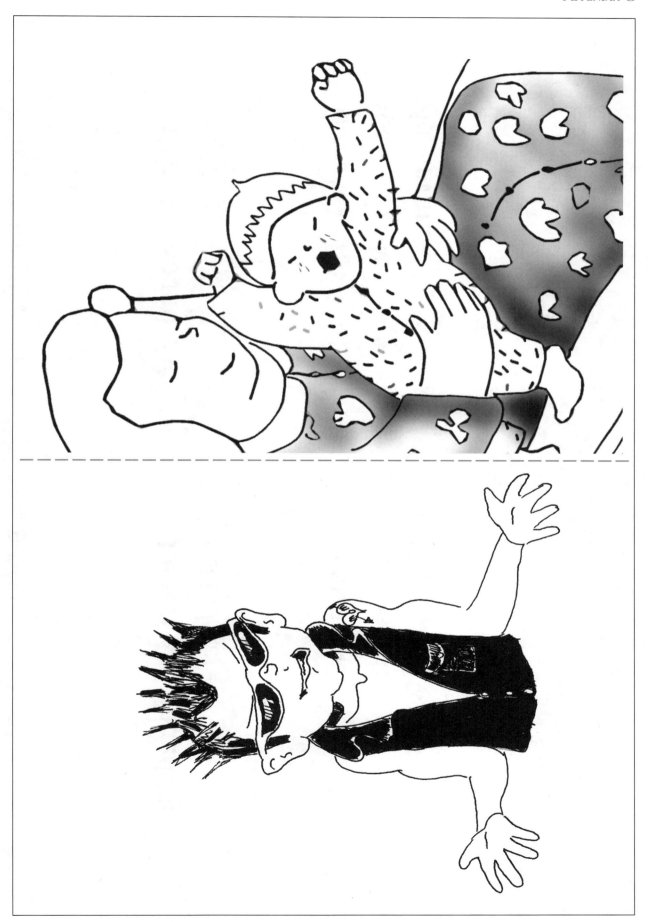

105 Crystal Springs Books (2003) **Reproducible**

Letter: Aa   Sound: /a/

(as in *bat*)

A, *a*, *a*,
Baby cries.
Rock her now.
Mommy tries.
a . . . a . . . a

- -

Letter: Aa   Sound: /ā/

(as in *lake*)

A, *a*, *a*,
Look at me.
I'm so cool,
Can't you see?
a . . . a . . . a

Letter: Bb Sound: /b/

Baby makes

A baby sound.

Baby's bottle

On the ground.

b . . . b . . . b

Letter: Hh Sound: /h/

Running hard,

Running fast,

Running race,

Running last.

h . . . h . . . h

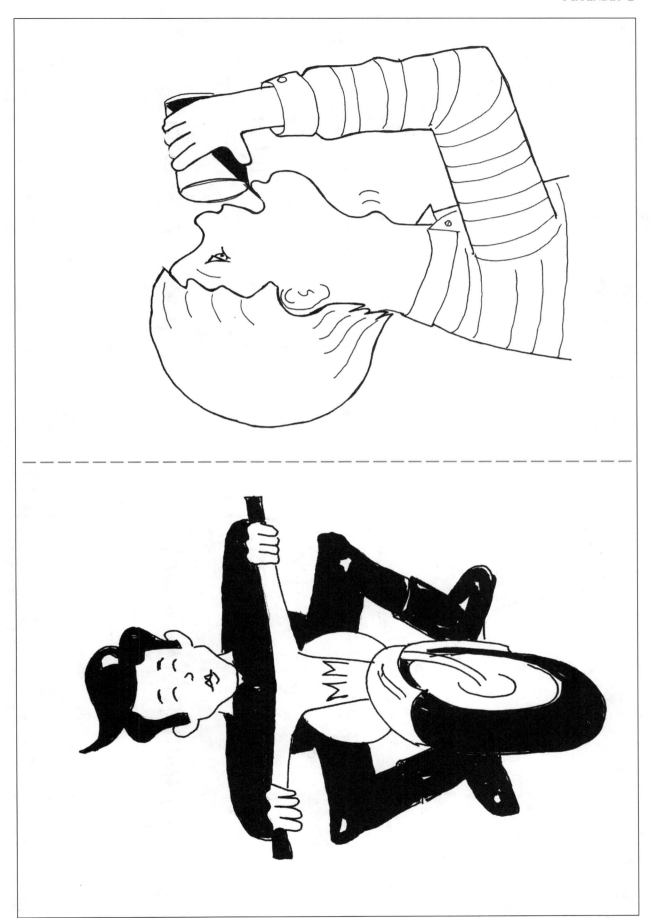

109 **Reproducible**

Letter: Gg Sound: /g/

Gulping, gulping,
Gulp it down.
Listen to that
Gurgle sound.

g . . . g . . . g

Letter: Vv Sound: /v/

Revin' up the motor.
Very nice bike.
Looking pretty cool,
Motorcycle Mike.

v . . . v . . . v

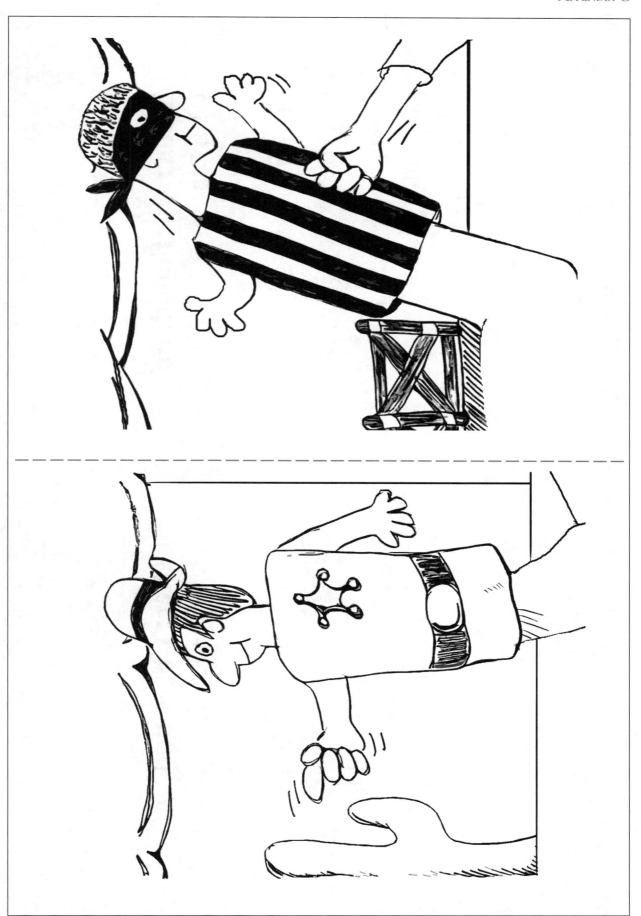

Letter: Uu Sound: /u/

(as in *up*)

Sheriff knocked him
On the ground.
Then he made a
Loud *uh* sound.

u . . . u . . . u

Letter: Uu Sound: /ū/

(as in *you*)

"You! You! You!
Bring back my horse."
The bad guy, he said,
"No!" of course.

u . . . u . . . u

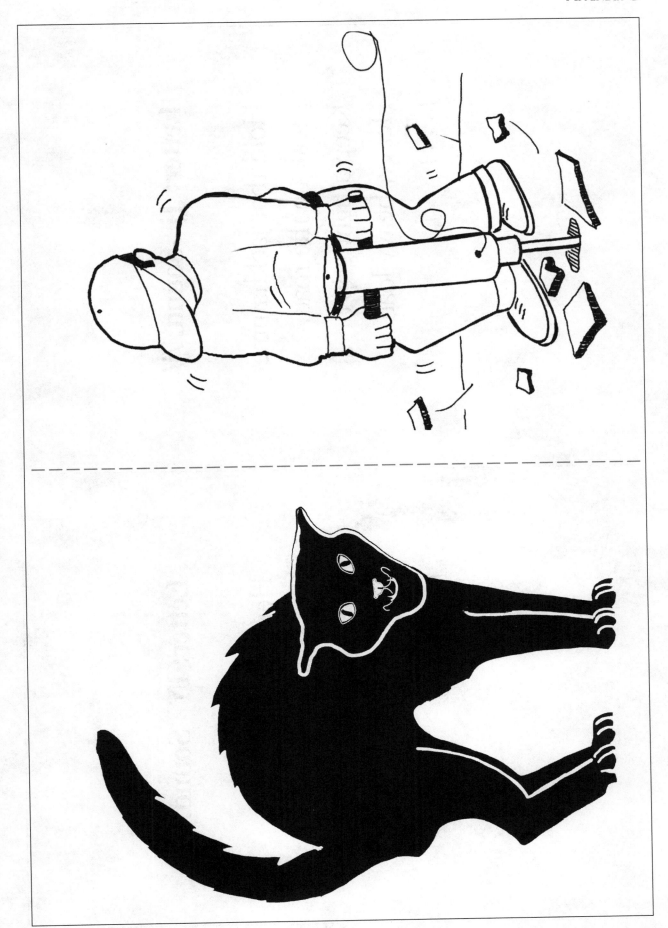

 Crystal Springs Books (2003) **Reproducible**

Letter: Jj   Sound: /j/

Hold that jackhammer,
Break up the road.
Keep a tight grip on a
Heavy, heavy load.

j . . . j . . . j

Letter: Ff   Sound: /f/

Here comes dog.
There goes cat.
Getting scared.
Hunched-up back.

f . . . f . . . f

115 **Reproducible**

Letter: Yy Sound: /y/

Little yuppy puppy,
Trying to get away.
"No, yuppy puppy,
Stay! Stay! Stay!"

y . . . y . . . y

Letter: Ww Sound: /w/

Window washing
At the store.
Windows, windows,
More and more.

w . . . w . . . w

116

Crystal Springs Books (2003)

Reproducible

Letter: Xx   Sound: /ks/

Bus comes by,
Stop, bus! Stop!
Rush, rush, rush,
Chop, chop, chop.

x . . . x . . . x

Letter: Qq   Sound: /kw/

Walking in the mud.
Mud is very deep.
Sticking in the mud.
Walking bare feet.

q . . . q . . . q

No More Letter of the Week   118   Crystal Springs Books (2003)   **Reproducible**

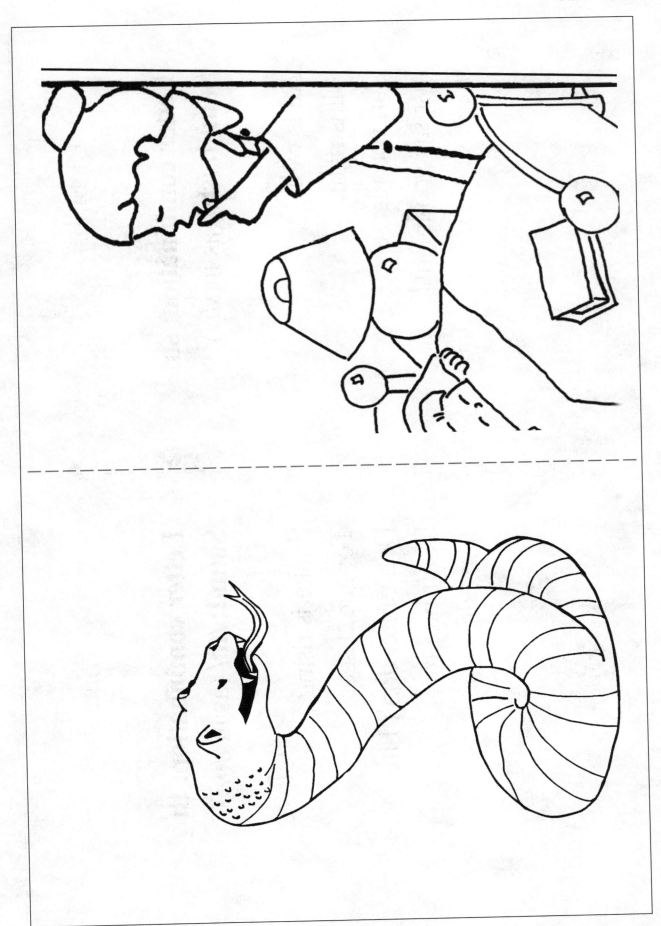

119

Reproducible

Digraphs

Letter combination: sh
Sound: /sh/ (as in *shy*)

All is well.

All is right.

Can you please

Just say goodnight?

sh . . . *sh* . . . *sh*

Digraphs

Letter combination: th
Sound: /th/ (as in *thin*)

Snake is rising.

Tongue, I see.

Don't bite, don't bite,

Don't bite me.

th . . . *th* . . . *th*

 Crystal Springs Books (2003)

Letter combination: wh
Sound: /wh/ (as in *whale*)

Blowing wind.
Hold your hat.
Too late now.
Hat! Come back.
wh . . . wh . . . wh . . . wh

Letter combination: ch
Sound /ch/ (as in *chin*)

Round the track,
Choo-choo train.
Round and round
And back again.
ch . . . ch . . . ch

Crystal Springs Books (2003) **Reproducible**

Sounds in A.c..t...i....o.....n!

Following are suggested actions that mimic the action illustrations and correspond to each rhyme represented on individual Sound Cards. Students will enjoy performing some of the actions in particular (such as pretending to spit seeds for the letter-sound /p/ or pretending to punch themselves in the stomach for the letter-sound /u/), but they should understand the importance of what I call "action etiquette," and be responsible.

Sound	Action
/r/	mean face of a growling dog
/ē/	arms flapping up and down, looking scared
/e/	fist (gently!) hitting mouth (like egg)
/s/	two hands making tire shape; tire goes flat as air escapes
/n/	arms out, flying like an airplane
/t/	pretending to drum with drumsticks
/ō/	mouth open, looking alarmed, hands at cheeks
/o/	mouth open, finger on tongue (like tongue depressor)
/k/	pretending to hammer a nail
/ī/	thumb pointing to chest
/i/	lifting foot as if stepped in something disgusting
/p/	pretending to spit
/d/	gently hitting forehead with heel of hand
/l/	wide open oval mouth, tongue behind front teeth, head tilting with each "lll" sound
/m/	mouth making the "mmm" sound, shutting eyes as if it is so delicious
/z/	pretending to swat at bees
/ā/	hands extended, palms up, raise shoulder as you say, "aaa"
/a/	crying like a baby

/h/	arms pumping, as if running
/b/	pointing to the floor, with sad baby face
/v/	pretending to rev up a motorcycle handlebar
/g/	pretending to guzzle a bottle of water
/ū/	pointing at someone
/u/	pretending to punch yourself in the stomach
/f/	arched back, angry cat face
/j/	pretending to work a jackhammer
/w/	using hand (like windshield wiper) to wash window
/y/	hand on neck (like leash would be choking puppy)
/kw/	walking, as if in deep mud
/ks/	pretending to step on the brakes and pull back a handle
/th/	arm weaving like snake with index and middle finger extended like the tongue (your tongue comes out when you make this sound)
/sh/	index finger over mouth, saying, "shhhhh"
/ch/	both arms, close to sides, making circles like wheels
/wh/	holding onto hat, swaying in the wind

Decoding Chart

	Nn	Uu	wh
Ff	Mm	Uu	th
Ee	Ll	Tt	sh
Ee	Kk	Ss	ch
Dd	Jj	Rr	Zz
Cc	Ii	Qq	Yy
Bb	Ii	Pp	Xx
Aa	Hh	Oo	Ww
Aa	Gg	Oo	Vv

Vowel Books

Written by Pat Lusche

Illustrations by
Phyllis Pittet

How to copy and use these book pages:

• Set your photocopier to copy pages double-sided.

• Photocopy each reproducible page for each individual Vowel Book (remember, last page and cover of each book appear on the same reproducible page). Be sure to configure each page in the right direction so text and illustrations will face the same direction on the final copy.

• When finished with one Vowel Book set, simply stack pages, face up, in order (last page and cover will appear as first reproducible page), fold along the dotted line, and staple.

NOTE: The reproducible Vowel Book pages have been set up for double-sided photocopying. If you choose not to tear out the reproducible pages to photocopy, experiment with the page placement on your photocopier.

How to use:

Remember to reproduce each Vowel Book emergent reader twice. One copy each belongs on the VSP's Reading Wall rectangle and the second copy belongs with the additional copies of the emergent readers in a tub for R/W Workshop times. You might consider creating a more durable front and back cover. Have students hand color the books!

Eggs for Breakfast

by Pat Lusche

This book belongs to

_____

Ee
/ē/ /e/

"Time to eat your eggs," said Andy's mom.

12

127

"You will not eat my eggs!"

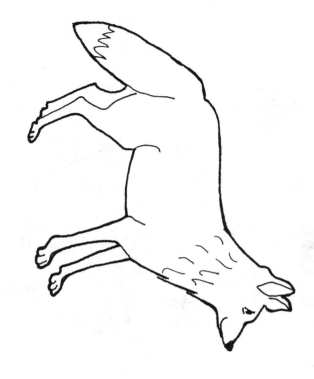

2

yelled Mama Snake.

11

yelled Mama Hen.

3

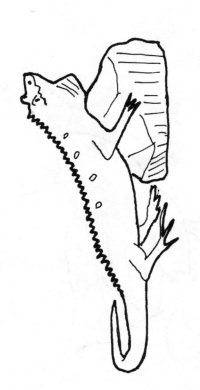

"You will not eat my eggs!"

10

"You will not eat my eggs!"

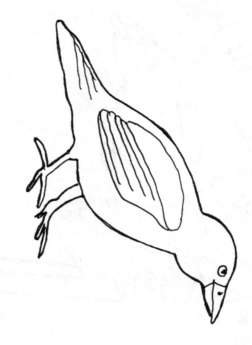

4

yelled Mama Goose.

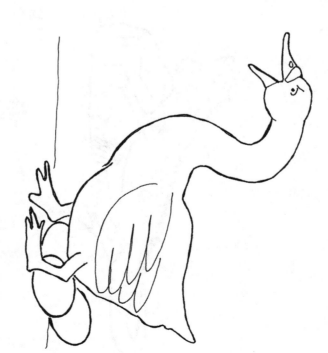

9

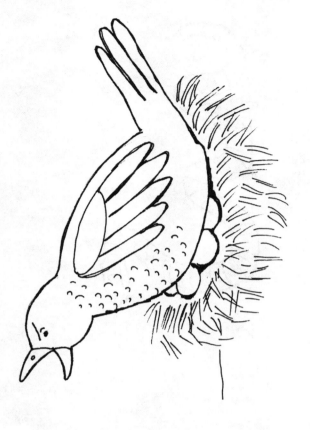

yelled Mama Bird.

5

"You will not eat my eggs!"

8

131

"You will not eat my eggs!"

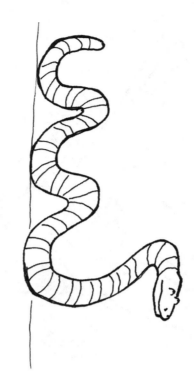

yelled Mama Turtle.

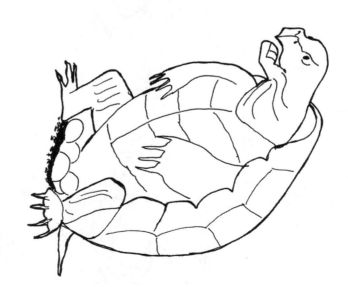

Not Oatmeal!

by Pat Lusche

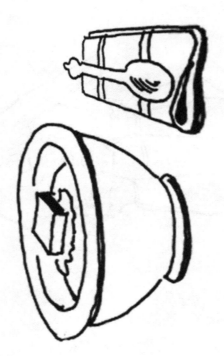

This book belongs to

_____

"I LOVE oatmeal!"

12

"I don't like oatmeal!"

2

Mom put chocolate syrup on
Molly's oatmeal.

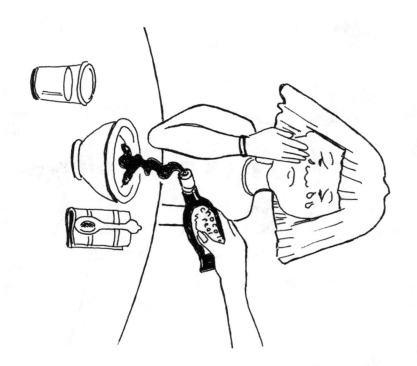

11

134

Mom put milk on Molly's
oatmeal.

3

"I don't like oatmeal!"

10

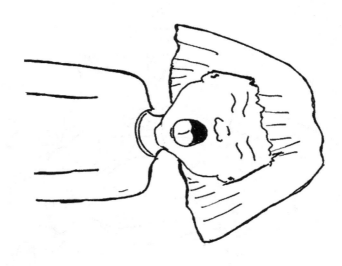

"I don't like oatmeal!"

4

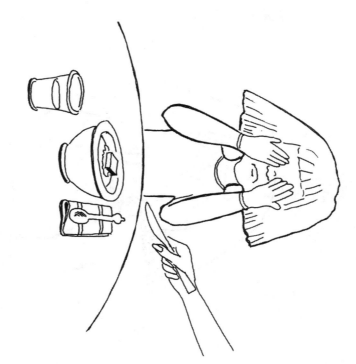

Mom put butter on Molly's oatmeal.

9

Mom put honey on Molly's oatmeal.

5

"I don't like oatmeal!"

8

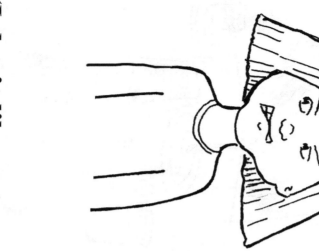

"I don't like oatmeal?"

6

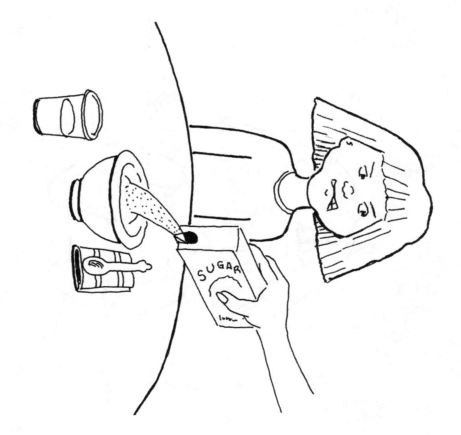

Mom put sugar on Molly's oatmeal.

7

Ice Cream

by Pat Lusche

This book belongs to

_____

Ii
/ĭ/ /ī/

8

Look! There is ice cream on her shoes.

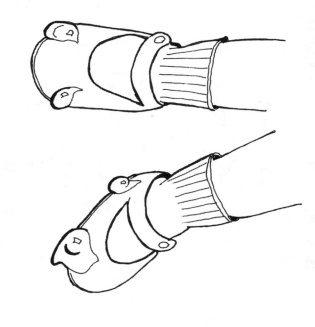

Is there any in her tummy, where it's supposed to be?

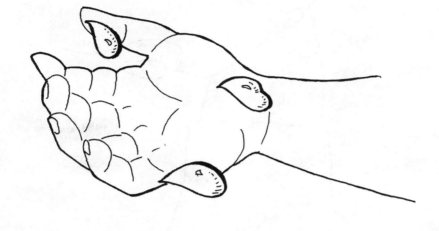

There is ice cream on her fingers.

3

There is ice cream on her knee.

6

There is ice cream on her arm.

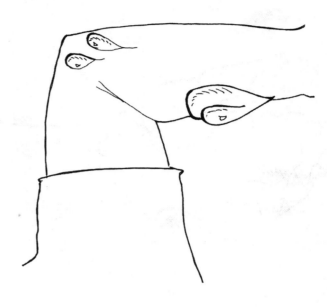

4

There is ice cream on her hair.

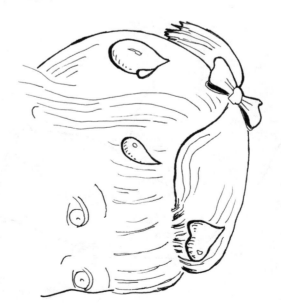

5

Please Smile

by Pat Lusche

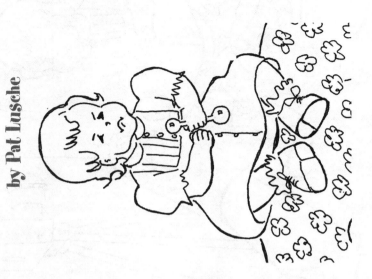

This book belongs to

_____

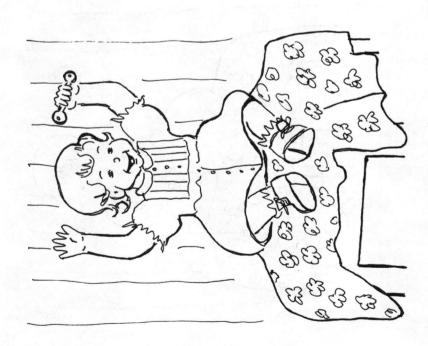

8

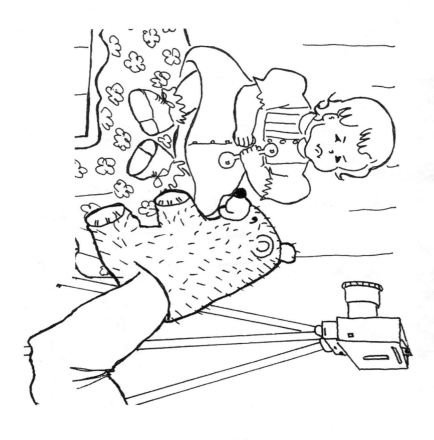

"Will you smile at the bear?"

2

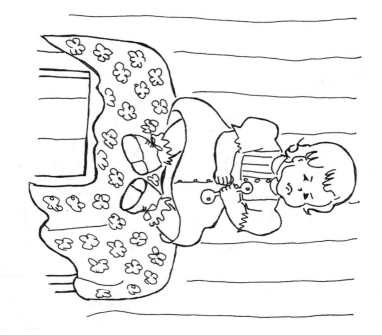

"I give up!"

7

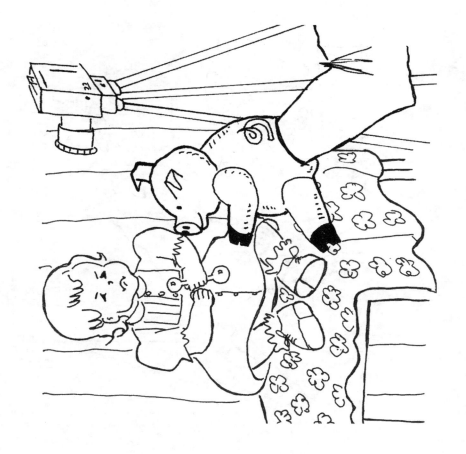

"Will you smile at the pig?"

3

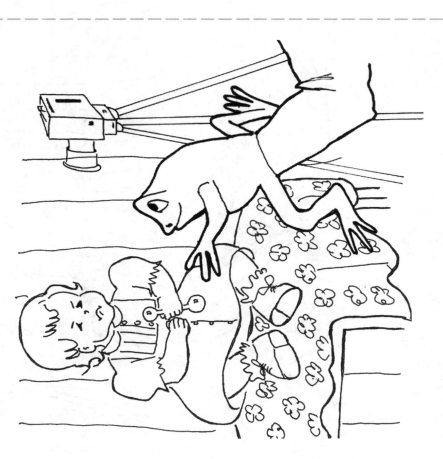

"Will you smile at the frog?"

6

"Will you smile at the dog?"

4

"Will you smile at the ape?"

5

Paint

by Pat Lusche

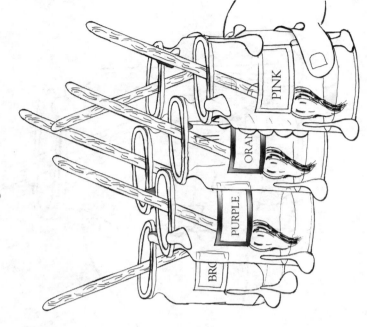

This book belongs to _____

"Here I am."

12

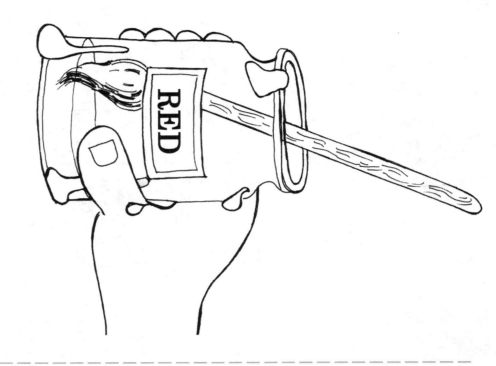

"Mom, Billy used up my
red paint

2

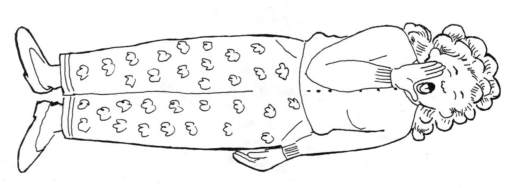

"Where is Billy?"

11

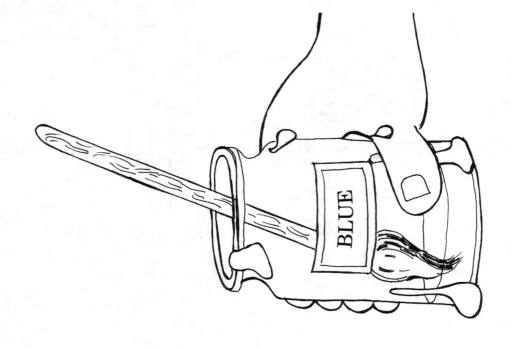

and my blue paint!"

3

**"Mom, Billy used up
all my paint!"**

10

"Mom, Billy used up my green paint

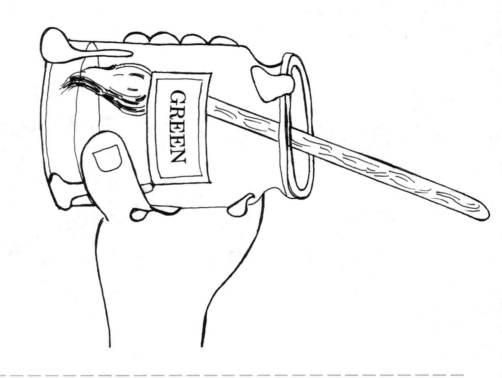

4

and my purple paint!"

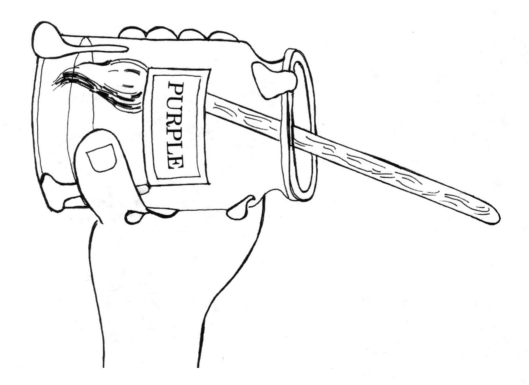

9

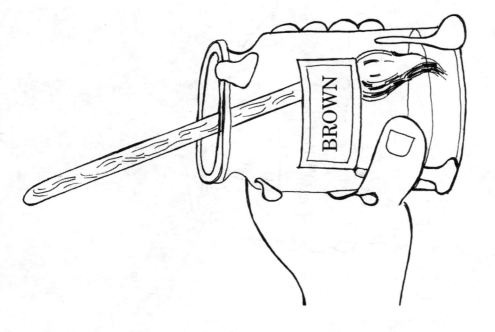

and my brown paint."

5

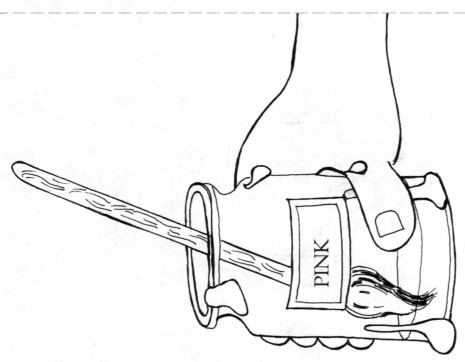

**"Mom, Billy used up my
pink paint**

8

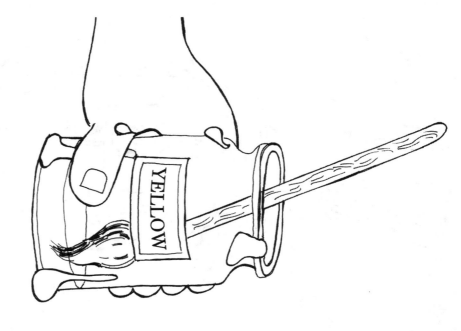

"Mom, Billy used up my
yellow paint

6

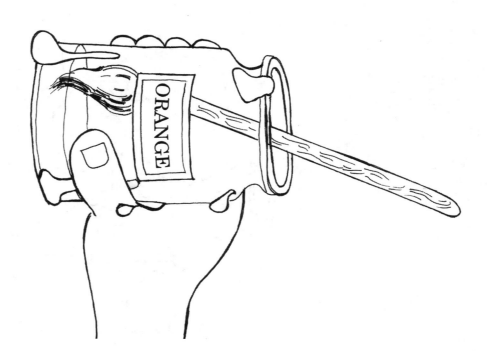

and my orange paint!"

7

152

Directions for Letter Formation

Saying the directions when forming letters often helps children learn their letters, while also improving their penmanship. You might choose to substitute words for *left* and *right*, if you are not teaching these concepts. For example, in the directions for lowercase *b*, you might say: From the top to the bottom/Up then around to the bottom, instead of: From the top to the bottom/Up and around to the right.

 Curve up to the top, then around to the bottom

 Curve up to the middle, then around to the bottom

 From the top to the bottom
From the top to the bottom
Across the middle

 Around in a circle
Up, then down

 Curve up to the top, then around to the bottom, then up
Across the middle

 Around in a circle to the left
Up, then down below the line, and make a left hook

 From the top to the bottom
Back to the top, then around and down

 Around in a circle to the left
Up to the top, then down to the bottom

 From the top
around to the bottom, then around to the top

 From the middle
around to the bottom, then around to the middle

 Around to the bottom, then around to the top
Add a small line

 Around in a circle to the left
Up, then down below the line, and make a small line up

From the top to the bottom
Across the top
Across the middle
Across the bottom

A line across
Up and over to the middle, then
around to the bottom

From the top to the bottom
From the top around to the
middle
Down to the bottom

From the middle to the bottom
Up and curve to the right

From the top to the bottom
From the top to the bottom
Slant top to bottom

From the middle to the bottom
Up, over, and down

From the top to the bottom
From the top to the bottom
Angle right toward the middle
Angle left toward the middle

From the middle to the bottom
Up, over, and down
Up, over, and down again

From the top to the bottom
From the top to the bottom
Across the middle

From the top to the bottom
Up, over, and down

From the top to the bottom
Around into the middle
Around to the bottom

From the top to the bottom
Up and around to the right

From the top to the bottom
From the top around to the
middle

From the middle straight
down past the line
Up, then around to the right

From the top to the bottom
Across the top
Across the middle

Curve around to the top, then
down to the bottom
Across the middle

Crystal Springs Books (2003)

From the top to the bottom
Across the top

Down to the bottom
Across the middle

From the top to the bottom
Across the bottom to the right

From the top to the bottom

From the top to the bottom
Across the top
Across the bottom

From the middle to the bottom,
then put a dot on top

From the top to the bottom
From the top to the middle
From the middle to the bottom

From the top to the bottom
From the middle in
Down to the bottom

From the top to the bottom,
then curve up to the left

Down from the middle, below
the line, and make a hook to
the left, then put a dot on top

Curve from the top to the
middle, then change direction
and curve down to the bottom
and up

Curve down from the middle,
then change direction and
curve down to the bottom
and up

From the top to the bottom,
then curve along the bottom
and back up to the top

From the middle to the
bottom, then curve back
up to the middle
Down to the bottom

Slant right, top to bottom
Slant left, top to bottom
Repeat for 3 and 4

Slant right, middle to bottom
Slant left, middle to bottom
Repeat for 3 and 4

Slant right, top to bottom
Slant left, top to the bottom

Slant right, middle to bottom
Slant left, middle to the bottom

Slant right, top to middle
Slant left, top to middle
Straight down to the bottom

Slant right, middle to bottom
Slant left from the middle,
then down below the line

Slant right, top to bottom
Slant left, top to bottom
 (the lines should cross in the middle)

Slant right, middle to bottom
Slant left, middle to bottom
 (the lines should cross in the middle)

Across the top, then
slant left top to bottom, then
across the bottom

Across the middle, then
slant left middle to bottom,
then across the bottom

 Crystal Springs Books (2003) **Reproducible**

Set I Sight Word List

Name: _____

a	I
am	is
to	in
like	come
go	see
me	it
here	this
and	look
my	the
at	we
up	on

Name: _____

a	I
am	is
to	in
like	come
go	see
me	it
here	this
and	look
my	the
at	we
up	on

Name: _____

a	I
am	is
to	in
like	come
go	see
me	it
here	this
and	look
my	the
at	we
up	on

Set 2 Sight Word List

Name: _____

jump	good
have	big
going	fast
she	saw
say	run
did	may
what	went
you	down
for	with
he	can
not	little
will	play

Name: _____

jump	good
have	big
going	fast
she	saw
say	run
did	may
what	went
you	down
for	with
he	can
not	little
will	play

Name: _____

jump	good
have	big
going	fast
she	saw
say	run
did	may
what	went
you	down
for	with
he	can
not	little
will	play

Set 3 Sight Word List

Name: _____

ride	funny
said	where
no	yes
sleep	very
then	do
but	are
who	so
after	get
from	eat
make	has
they	was
read	some

Name: _____

ride	funny
said	where
no	yes
sleep	very
then	do
but	are
who	so
after	get
from	eat
make	has
they	was
read	some

Name: _____

ride	funny
said	where
no	yes
sleep	very
then	do
but	are
who	so
after	get
from	eat
make	has
they	was
read	some

Notebook Page Directions

- Photocopy the notebook page reproducible (see page 161) 26 times.

- At the bottom of each notebook page, type in the appropriate sentence for each letter-sound. The type size and letter style should be legible and appropriate for young readers. (Hint: Simply type each sentence on the computer at the bottom of a blank document page. Run the 26 reproducible notebook pages through the printer so the appropriate sentence prints out on the bottom of the coinciding notebook page.)

- Photocopy the Decoding Chart (see page 125) and cut out each letter square. Paste the appropriate illustration in the box at the top of each page.

- Photocopy (one at a time) the appropriate number of each notebook page for your class.

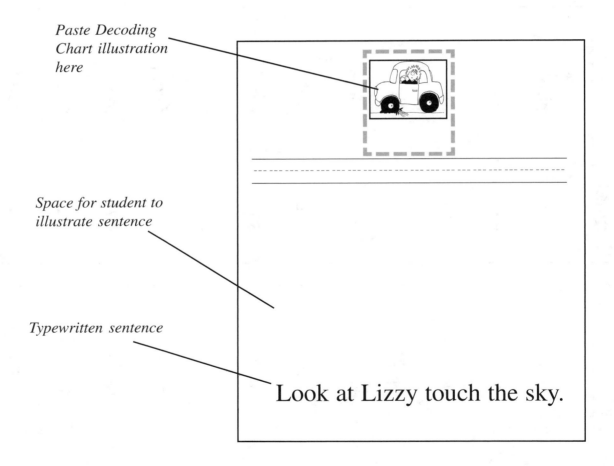

Paste Decoding Chart illustration here

Space for student to illustrate sentence

Typewritten sentence

Look at Lizzy touch the sky.

Build-a-Sentence

Name: _____

Reading Procedure

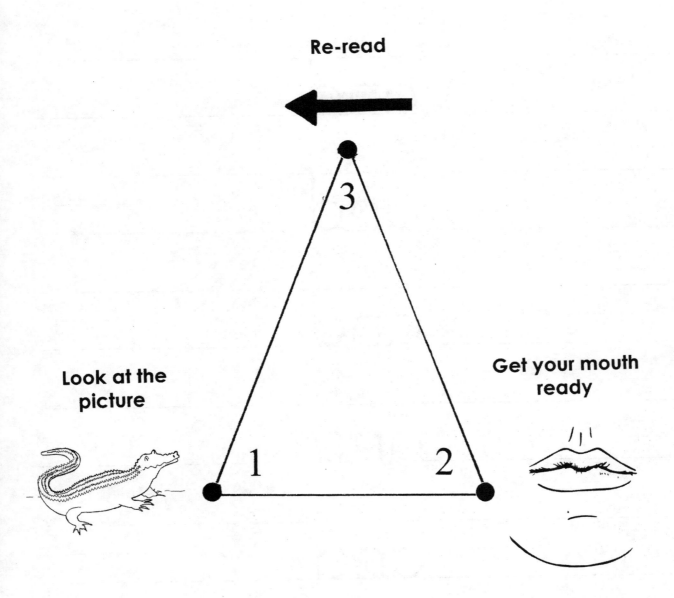

Re-read

3

Look at the picture

Get your mouth ready

1

2

Name: _____

These Words Rhyme!

and

and

and

and

and

and

Name: _____

2-letter words

3-letter words

4-letter words

165

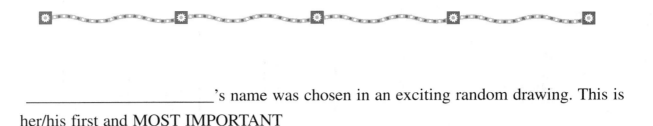

_____'s name was chosen in an exciting random drawing. This is her/his first and MOST IMPORTANT

Home-School Assignment

for the entire kindergarten year. Your child will be the "Letter-Sound Expert" for the letter ____ and will assist her/his classmates in becoming experts too!

Please help your child to:

1. Recognize the letter, both uppercase and lowercase.

2. Write the letter, both uppercase and lowercase.

3. Tell what sound the letter makes.

4. Read the following sentence, touching each word while reading:

_____

5. Bring something that will fit in a sandwich bag that starts with your child's letter (Example: Rr: ring, rubber band, rice). This will be stapled to the Reading Wall all year long.

6. Try to do all this by tomorrow!

In the meantime, I will be working with your child to read the book her/his sentence came from. Your child's picture will be placed by her/his letter on the Reading Wall. After successfully completing this homework assignment, s/he will serve as a resource for other children for the entire year.

Thank you for all your help!

Sincerely,

 # Sight Word Support

Dear Parents,

Thanks for faithfully working on the sentences with your child every night. It is such a powerful five minutes.

I am sending home the attached list of sight words. These are words your child knows "by sight." S/he should not have to think about them or sound them out. Most children focused on learning to read are very eager to pick up these "islands of certainty" when they swim around in this sea of reading. Please use your own discretion about the amount of time you wish to spend on these words. If your daughter or son shows little interest, persevere—move slowly, but keep it fun.

When your child is learning a new sight word, you might want to have her/him practice writing it in salt. Shoebox lids filled with salt work great. You could also try shaving cream on your kitchen table. MagnaDoodle, chalkboards, Dad's tummy, frosty windows, and foggy mirrors are fun and exciting, too. Or try spelling words with your eyes shut, circling them in the newspaper, looking for them in books—whatever your creative mind can come up with to keep your child motivated.

Your daughter/son has a copy of these same sight words written on Punch Cards and located on the Reading Wall (by your child's alphabet letter) in the classroom. A volunteer will come in once a week and check the sight words, punching holes by words your daughter/son knows. These words are available for your child to look at when s/he writes. If your child can read it, I will expect her/him to use "book spelling" (correct spelling) when writing in her/his journals. Not all students are ready for this level of work, but I'm finding many can build quite an impressive sight-word vocabulary prior to entering first grade.

Thanks for all your support with this, and again, use your own best judgment about the amount of time you want to spend on sight words; follow the lead of your child.

Thanks again,

Completed Assignment Sheet

Date	Name of Book	Parent Signature/Comments

 **Nightly Sentence**

_____'s Homework

Dear Parents:

In an effort to help your child progress more quickly in reading and writing, I am asking that you write with your child for five minutes each night.

Together, write a sentence of your child's choice. Help her/him
_s . . . t . . . r . . . e . . . t . . . c . . . h_ the sounds. You write while your child listens for the sounds. Write one sentence each school night in "book spelling" (correct spelling). Let your student tell you the sounds s/he hears, and you supply all the other sounds. Your daughter/son will consistently see you model the sounds s/he doesn't know and soon enough s/he will know them, too! If your child knows all her/his sounds, s/he will nonetheless benefit by learning other important components to our language system and how it works.

Please put five sentences on each page of the homework book and send the book to class with your child on:

____Tuesday

____Wednesday

____Thursday

Thanks for all you do!

Sincerely,

Resources

Bibliography

Allington, Richard L. *What Really Matters for Struggling Readers: Designing Research-Based Programs.* Boston, Mass: Addison-Wesley, 2001.

Baratta-Lorton, Robert. *Baratta-Lorton Reading Program: Teacher's Manual.* Saratoga, Calif.: Center for Innovation in Education, 1985.

Benson, Laura. *Colorado Reads!* Denver, Colo.: Colorado Department of Education, 2000.

———. "Strategy Collections for Growing Readers and Writers. . . and Their Growing Teachers." Denver, Colo.: *The Colorado Communicator,* 2002.

Clay, Marie M. *Becoming Literate/The Construction of Inner Control.* Portsmouth, N.H.: Heinemann, 1991.

———. *An Observation Survey of Early Literacy Achievement.* Auckland, New Zealand: Heinemann, 1993.

———. *By Different Paths to Common Outcomes.* York, Maine: Stenhouse, 1998.

Dixon-Krauss, Lisbeth. *Vygotsky in the Classroom.* White Plains, N.Y.: Longman Publishers USA, 1996.

Dolch, Edward W. *The 2000 Commonest Words for Spelling: Revised According to the Latest Scientific Studies.* Champaign, Ill.: Garrard Publishing Co., 1955.

Dole, J. A., G. Duffy, L. Roehler, and P. D. Pearson. "Moving from the Old to the New: Research on Comprehension Instruction." *Review of Educational Research* 61 (summer 1991): 239–264.

Fountas, Irene C., and Gay Su Pinnell. *Guided Reading: Good First Teaching for All Children.* Portsmouth, N.H.: Heinemann, 1996.

Holdaway, Don. *Foundations of Literacy.* Portsmouth, N.H.: Heinemann, 1979.

Pearson, P. David. "Focus on Research, Teaching and Learning Reading: A Research Perspective." *Language Arts* 70 (1993): 502–511.

Richardson, Jan, keynote speaker. Annual Leadership in Literacy Conference. Cherry Creek School District, Aurora, Colo., 2000.

Stephens, D. S. *Research on Whole Language: Support for a New Curriculum.* New York: Richard C. Owens, 1991.

Vygotsky, L. S. *Mind in Society: The Development of Higher Psychological Processes.* Edited by M. Cole, V. John Steiner, S. Scribner, and E. Souberman. Cambridge, Mass.: Harvard University Press, 1978.

———. *Thought and Language.* Edited by A. Kozulin. Cambridge, Mass.: MIT Press, 1986.

A Selection of Children's Books Mentioned in the Text

Cannon, Janell. *Stellaluna.* San Diego, Calif.: Harcourt Brace Jovanovich, 1993.

Cowley, Joy. *The Farm Concert.* Bothell, Wash.: The Wright Group, 1998.

———. *Hairy Bear.* San Diego, Calif.: The Wright Group, 1980.

————. *Meanies*. Auckland, New Zealand: Shortland Publications Limited, 1983.

————. *The Monster's Party*. San Diego, Calif.: The Wright Group. 1984.

————. *Mrs. Wishy-Washy*. Bothell, Wash.: The Wright Group, 1980.

Johnson, Paul Brett. *The Cow Who Wouldn't Come Down*. New York: Orchard Books, 1993.

Lewison, Wendy Cheyette. *Going to Sleep on the Farm*. New York: Trumpet Club, Inc., 1992.

Lusche, Pat. *The Inside Story*. San Diego, Calif.: Dominie Press, Inc., 1996.

Melser, June, and Joy Cowley. *In a Dark, Dark Wood*. Bothell, Wash.: The Wright Group, 1998.

Penn, Audrey. *The Kissing Hand*. Washington, D.C.: Child Welfare League of America, Inc., 1993.

Polacco, Patricia. *My Rotten Redheaded Older Brother*. New York: Simon & Schuster Books for Young Readers, 1994.

Wood, Audrey. *The Napping House*. Orlando, Fla.: Harcourt Brace Jovanovich, 1984.

Emergent-Level Book Publishers/Distributors

Creative Teaching Press, Inc.
P.O. Box 6017
Cypress, CA 90630-0017
Phone: (714) 995-7888
Fax: (714) 995-5173
Web: www.creativeteaching.com

Dominie Press, Inc.
5945 Pacific Center Boulevard,
Suite 505
San Diego, CA 92121
Phone: (800) 232-4570
Fax: (619) 546-8822
Web: www.dominie.com

Kaeden Corp.
P.O. Box 16190
Rocky River, OH 44116
Phone: (216) 333-9981
Fax: (216) 356-5081
Web: www.kaeden.com

Modern Curriculum Press
P.O. Box 2649
Columbus, OH 43216
Phone: (800) 321-3106
Fax: (614) 771-7362
Web: www.pearsonlearning.com

Rigby Education
P.O. Box 797
Crystal Lake, IL 60039
Phone: (800) 822-8661
Fax: (800) 427-4429
Web: www.rigby.com

Scholastic, Inc.
2931 East McCarty Street
Jefferson City, MO 65101
Phone: (800) 724-6527
Fax: (573) 635-5881
Web: www.scholastic.com

Seedling Publications, Inc.
4079 Overlook Drive East
Columbus, OH 43214-2931
Phone: (614) 451-2412
Fax: (614) 742-0786
Web: www.seedlingpub.com

Steck-Vaughn Co.
P.O. Box 26015
Austin, TX 78755
Phone: (800) 531-5015
Web: www.steck-vaughn.com

Sundance Publishing
P.O. Box 26015
Littleton, MA 01460
Phone: (800) 343-8204
Fax: (508) 486-1053
Web: www.sundancepub.com

Sunshine Books
413 Great South Rd.
Penrose, Auckland, New Zealand 1005
Web: www.sunshine.com.nz

The Wright Group Publishing
19201 120th Avenue NE
Bothell, WA 98011
Phone: (800) 523-2371
Fax: (800) 543-7323
Web: www.wrightgroup.com

Zaner-Bloser Educational Publishers
2200 West Fifth Ave.
P.O. Box 16764
Columbus, OH 43216-6764
Phone: (800) 421-3018
Fax: (800) 992-6087
Web: www.zaner-bloser.com

Alphabet books and accompanying pictures:

Resources for Reading
P.O. Box 5783
Redwood City, CA 94063
Phone: (800) ART-READ
Web: www.abcstuff.com

Rhyming pictures:

Lakeshore Learning Materials
2695 E. Dominquez
P.O. Box 6261
Carson, CA 90749
Phone: (800) 421-5354
Web: www.lakeshorelearning.com